The World As It Was When Jesus Came

The World
As It Was
When
Jesus Came

A Companion to the New Testament

Dr. Mark Hopkins

ARPress
ILLUMINATING IDEAS
EMPOWERING VOICES

ARPress
45 Dan Road Suite 5
Canton MA 02021

Hotline:	1(888) 821-0229
Fax:	1(508) 545-7580

Ordering Information:

Quantity sales. Special discounts are available on quantity purchases by corporations, associations, and others. For details, contact the publisher at the address above.

Printed in the United States of America.

ISBN-13:	Softcover	979-8-89356-507-2
	eBook	979-8-89356-508-9

Library of Congress Control Number: 2024902499

CONTENTS

FOREWORD

Fifty years of reading the Bible and teaching from its pages have convinced me that a true understanding of God's word cannot be achieved without first having an understanding of the history of the times and other factors that affected the people who were writing the scriptures. To many students of the New Testament, the environment of the Christian gospel is an unknown world. They read it only in the light of their own time and interpret it by their own experience. In reality, the New Testament was written for a culture that has long since passed out of existence and for patterns of thought that often are not remembered or understood by the modern world. To reach an understanding of the scriptures it is necessary to look closely at the history of that time just before the birth of Christ and to the political and social realities of the people who were both the writers and the readers of those first books of the New Testament.

This book, *The World as It Was When Jesus Came,* is designed as a resource and support text for the study of the New Testament. It provides an overview of the history of Biblical times. It is not intended to be a theological text. Instead, its purpose is to provide a context through which the reader can better understand the message of the scriptures, who wrote them, and why. The early portions focus on the historical context, geography and language translation that affects our understanding of the Bible. The latter portion provides an overview and synopsis of the books of the New Testament. The Appendix provides several essays on a wide range of subjects that can best be described as linking history with scripture. With such links it is inevitable that speculations may become a part of the presentation. These may come either from Bible scholars or the author. Included are such subjects as

The Case for Mark the Gospel Writer as a Dual Citizen of Jerusalem and Rome, The Treatment of Women in the Bible, The Contributions of Paul the Apostle, and other topics that may be of interest to the reader.

Several people were helpful in writing and editing this book. These include professional editor and friend Kathryn Smith, who helped to make the contents readable and kept me on track regarding the purpose of the book. The ministers who served as readers, Doctors Paul Talmadge, Randall Ruble, and Jack Ellenburg, each provided insight into the theological and historical content. Publisher's agent Les Stobbe read parts of the manuscript and provided guidance regarding presentation of material. Most significant is my wife, Ruth, who critiques everything I write and often has some advice that adds texture to the content and makes it hit closer to home.

The book is divided into four sections with each having its own purpose. An explanation of each division follows.

SETTING THE STAGE

What was the political, social, and geographic world Jesus entered more than 2,000 years ago? Between the last of the prophets of the Old Testament and the advent of Christ recorded in the four Gospels lies a period virtually unknown to most, and yet of great importance in understanding the scriptures. The events of that period are extremely important because they formed the political and religious environment in which the earliest Christian faith developed.

TELLING THE STORY OF JESUS

The four Gospels, Matthew, Mark, Luke, and John, focus on the life of Jesus as seen from the perspective of the Gospel writers. They told the story of Jesus but also gave insights into their own lives, their purpose for writing, and the unique window through which they watched the story unfold. This text explores the many influences on their lives just before and during the time they were sharing their perspectives on the life and times of Jesus through the Gospels they wrote.

SPREADING THE WORD

Many people played a role in spreading the word of Jesus Christ and the New Covenant to the known world of that time. These included the original Apostles such as Matthew, Peter, and John as well as those who became followers later such as Paul, Barnabas, Mark, Timothy, and a host of others. Included in this section is an overview of the thirteen letters written by Paul, along with the letters and messages from Peter, John, James, Titus, Jude, and the book of prophesy called Revelation written by John. In each case the synopsis of each New Testament book opens with descriptions of the who, what, when, why, and where of the books as a whole, as well as several of the major scriptures from each book. The purpose is to give the reader a quick overview of the contents of the writings of each of the authors and the primary message they convey.

APPENDIX

The dictionary says that an appendix is material attached to the end of a manuscript that may supplement or add to the understanding of the text. This appendix is a series of essays and supplemental information on a variety of subjects that may be of interest to the reader. The intent of this section is to share some information on questions that are raised when you match history with the scriptures. There are many mysteries in the Bible. History can shed light on some of the mysteries and can generate speculations about others. It is hoped that the essays and other additions will be of interest to the reader.

SECTION I

THE EFFECTS OF HISTORICAL CONTEXT, GEOGRAPHY, AND LANGUAGE TRANSLATION ON OUR UNDERSTANDING OF THE BIBLE

Reading the Bible is basic to understanding God's message to mankind. Unfortunately, many factors influence our understanding as we read God's word. The King James Bible is familiar to most, and was written in English translated from the Hebrew, Aramaic, or Greek in which it was originally written. However, for full understanding, we must be able to place the events and happenings in the context of the times in which they occurred. How did the conquests of Alexander the Great affect the spread of the gospel? How did the way the Romans governed their empire affect Paul the Apostle and other Christian missionaries as they traveled throughout the world of that time?

From time to time we hear the words, "The Bible says it, I believe it, and that settles it." It is a simple expression, one that many people can relate to. Unfortunately, it can be compared to the childhood chant, "Sticks and stone may break my bones but names will never hurt me." We know from experience that the "sticks and stones" statement just isn't true. Names can hurt and sometimes they shape lives in ways that are not intended and that make existence much more difficult. In order for the "I believe it" statement about the Bible to be viable, we must first be able to establish what the Bible is saying to us. That requires us to understand the written and spoken language of the original text as well as the issues implicit in translation. Once we have an understanding of the words, then what we believe can become the focus. Of course, once the words are understood, what an individual believes is directly dependent on each person's life experiences and the foundations for understanding in that individual's mind.

Reading the text of the Bible is not enough. The reader must understand what he has read and be able to activate God's word in his daily life. Being able to put the word of God and the teachings of Jesus into practice is directly related to the extent to which we can relate to "translated" language and to the reader's field of reference--the history from which our ability to understand is drawn.

THE IMPORTANCE OF HISTORY

The focus of history is the ascent of mankind, from the beginning to today. Using history to supplement the scriptures is a legitimate way to fill in the blanks of scripture and, conversely, to fill in the blanks of history. This helps the reader know and understand not only the lessons of the scriptures but also the pressures on the people and what was going on in the region and country where they lived at the time.

There are some significant omissions in scripture. The scriptures tell us that Jesus visited the Temple in Jerusalem when he was twelve years of age. Once he returned home the scriptures are silent on his life until he begins his ministry in the Synagogue in Nazareth when he was thirty. What occurred in Jesus' life during those silent eighteen years? There is an additional "silent" period between the end of the Book of Nehemiah (423 B.C.) and the birth of Christ, assumed to be in 5 B.C.

The role of women is an issue of controversy both in the Bible and today, yet Jesus never addressed the issue of the status of women. Slavery is another major issue. Approximately half of the population in the Roman Empire was made up of slaves, and yet Jesus never addressed the social condition of slavery.

How can we understand the historical background of such social issues in history and in scripture? How can the gaps in the scriptures be understood and the lack of focus on these key issues be explained without making assumptions or speculations and, perhaps, assuming what is not there? The answer is in linking history and ethnic traditions with the scriptures to gain a more complete picture of what was happening in Bible times.

The Bible was written in the context of the Hebrew Nation and the Jewish culture. It was written primarily by Jews and much of it was written *for* Jews. We must understand Judaism and Jewish culture in order to understand what is written into the New Covenant between God and his people.

History tells us that the Hebrew people were among the most educated of the various people of that time and that they educated both male and female children. How were the children educated and who was responsible for their education? How were the rituals of Judaism carried out and how were the rules of Judaism enforced? What was the structure of the Jewish family? How did all of this affect those living and writing the scriptures in Biblical times?

The scriptures were written by many different writers, inspired by the spirit mind of God, and presented together in a mosaic of history, music, poems, stories, and directions for living. All writers of the Bible were real people of their times, with the normal human circumstances of family, work, religion, and government, just like today. Knowing the history and traditions of the time helps us to understand the pressures and influences on writers of the scriptures.

The blanks in scripture can never be fully filled in without divine revelation. However, our perspectives can be broadened and insights can be gained not only into *what* happened but *why* if we link our knowledge and understanding of history with our study of the scriptures.

HOW GEOGRAPHY AFFECTS THE SCRIPTURES

There is no doubt that geography affects history in a variety of ways, and it certainly affected the scriptures. The annual range of temperature, elevation of the land, amount of rainfall, distance from the equator, whether the land is mountainous, flat, or a flood plain, and the relative distances from place to place, all have an effect on the history of a region. Key also is the availability of natural resources and the location of the country in relation to other countries.

In modern times, countries like Singapore and Panama are important to the economic well-being of their regions because of their location. Each sits at a key point where trade routes cross. The circumstances of modern countries such as Saudi Arabia, India, the United States, and Russia are greatly affected by geography. Of these four countries, the U.S. has the greatest variety of natural resources, from fertile farm land to oil fields to coal and copper mines. Saudi Arabia has much of the world's reserves of oil, but little else. India has no oil at all. Russia, with limited natural resources, has now harnessed its oil reserves but, for many years, had designs on the natural resources of its neighbors to supplement meager resources available in the home country. This is the main reason for the creation of the Soviet Union which, after the fall of old imperial Russia, was a quest for raw materials to allow the Soviets to compete economically in the modern world. Today, many of the countries of the Middle East are important to the rest of the world because of their oil resources.

Unfortunately, Israel is a country in the Middle East that has few natural resources. Its importance in Biblical times related primarily to the location of trade routes between the dominant countries of that period in history.

In Genesis of the Old Testament we can read the story of Abraham who lived in Ur on the Euphrates River in the region of present-day Kuwait. He moved his family and all of his possessions at God's direction. (Please note the travels of Abraham in the map section.)

> *The Lord said to Abraham: Go out from your land, your relatives, and your father's house to the land that I will show you. I will make you into a great nation, I will bless you, I will make your name great, and you will be a blessing. (Genesis 12: 1-2)*

Kuwait is at the eastern edge of what geographers call the Fertile Crescent. This crescent is a narrow strip of land that runs from present-day Kuwait north up the Tigris and Euphrates River valleys and then back south through the land bordered by the Mediterranean and the Jordan River, what we refer to today as the Holy Land. The Fertile Crescent gets its name from the shape of this fertile strip of land.

TRADE ROUTES THROUGH THE HOLY LAND

The Holy Land is a place that is important to the history of the world because it is the place where three of the major religions of the world originated, but it is also important because of the trade routes that ran within its borders. Between 2000 B.C. and 1000 A.D., a period of 3,000 years, this little strip of land along the eastern coast of the Mediterranean Sea became the focal point of the trade that went on between all the major countries of the Middle East. (Please note the map of trade routes in the map section.)

During Biblical times, there were five major civilizations that developed in the region. To the north of the Holy Land in present-day Turkey and northern Iraq were the Assyrians. To the west were Greece and its city-states, and further west was Rome. To the east were the Babylonian Empire and its predecessors and successors. To the south was Egypt. All of the more northern civilizations wanted to trade with Egypt, which was located to the south at the gateway to the vast continent of Africa. In order for any of these countries to reach Egypt for trade, political, or military purposes they had to travel through the Holy Land.

When God moved Abraham from Ur on the Euphrates River in present-day Kuwait to the center of the Holy Land, He was moving him and his family to the center of trade and commerce in the Middle East. He could not have placed him at a more important location for the spread of the Jewish and later the Christian religions. At the same time, He could not have placed Abraham at any location in the world where there was more conflict, wars, and rumors of wars, both then and now. Those dominant trade routes had to run along the eastern shore of the Mediterranean Sea because of the impassible desert to the east and the volatile sea to the west. Wherever you lived in relation to the Holy Land--whether north, south, east, or west--any trade route you used was going to take you through the Holy Land. Trade routes are still important today though Israel no longer plays the key role of location as it did 2,000 years ago. In Biblical times there was constant conflict between those dominant countries for control of the mid-eastern trade routes and the Holy Land through which they passed.

THE DEAD SEA RIFT

The Bible makes constant references to the geography of the region. The fact that Israel's eastern border runs along a natural division that was created by the movement of the Arabian and African Tectonic Plates several million years ago is very important. The result is the Dead Sea Rift that stretches northward from the Red Sea to Mount Herman north of the Sea of Galilee. At its lower end at the Dead Sea, the rift is 1,300 feet below sea level, the lowest land mass anywhere in the world. The northern area of the rift is home to the Jordan River that flows from the mountains into the Sea of Galilee and then south through the Jordan Valley. That valley is home to Jericho, one of the oldest cities in the world. Much of the history of the Holy Land happened along the Dead Sea Rift, whether in the rift itself or in the cities that bordered the rift. (Please note the maps of the Dead Sea Rift in the map section.)

THE SEA OF GALILEE

The Sea of Galilee is just eleven miles long and seven miles wide, yet it sits at the center of much of Biblical history. The feeding of the five thousand, the casting out of demons, the Sermon on the Mount, and nine miracles all happened on its shores. It is known for sudden storms, and these are caused by several unique aspects of geography. (Please note the map of the Sea of Galilee in the map section.)

There are four factors that affect the weather on the Sea of Galilee. First, the elevation of the sea is 695 feet below sea level. Second, the range of mountains that rim this inland body of water are up to

2,000 feet in height. The third factor is the close proximity of the Mediterranean Sea, which is less than 50 miles west of the Sea of Galilee, and the fourth is the direction of the prevailing winds in the region, which are west to east.

During six months of the year, October to March, the Mediterranean Sea is volatile. During that six-month period the sea was impassable for the round-bottom boats that were used for transport along the coast of the Mediterranean and on the Sea of Galilee. The winds were too strong and cold for safety. When those winds reach the Holy Land on the eastern shore of the Mediterranean Sea, the cold air is pushed upward to the 2,000-foot elevation of the mountain ridge that is on the west side of the Sea of Galilee. The map of the region shows the features of the mountain geography that are important to the forming of storms on the Sea of Galilee. First, because of the way the mountain ridge is shaped, it creates a funnel on the west side of the ridge, thus channeling the cold air into a thick wave. Second, on the side of the ridge nearest the Sea of Galilee, there is a second natural funnel that, along with gravity (cold air is heavier than warm air), channels the cold air forcefully down the mountain slope more than 2,600 feet into the northern section of the sea.

Without the benefit of weather satellites or other more modern methods of predicting the weather, the small fishing boats of the northern portion of the Sea of Galilee were victims of every change in the weather that brought a cold gusting wind down from the mountain ridge 2,600-plus feet above them. One of the best known stories of the Bible comes from a Sea of Galilee storm.

A fierce windstorm arose, and the waves were breaking over the boat, so that the boat was already being swamped. . . He got up, rebuked the wind, and said to the sea, "Silence, be still." The wind ceased, and there was a great calm. . . And they were terrified and asked one another, "Who then is this? Even the wind and the sea obey Him!" (Mark 4: 37, 39, 41)

FARM LANDS AND THE MOUNTAIN RIDGE

The geography of the Holy Land is dominated by a ridge of mountains that runs from Mount Hermon in the north to the edge of the Sinai Desert at the south along the Dead Sea Rift. There are two valleys that provide most of the farmland that feeds the population. They are the Jordan River Valley that runs along the eastern border of the country and the Jezreel Valley that runs east and west from the Sea of Galilee to the Mediterranean. (Note the map of the Jordan and Jezreel Valleys in the map section.) Jerusalem sits on top of Mt. Zion, one of the highest elevations in the country. Thus, the often read reference in the Bible about going "up to Jerusalem" is because Jerusalem was "up" from almost every location in the Holy Land.

THE EFFECTS OF LANGUAGE ON UNDERSTANDING THE SCRIPTURES

In the late 1970s President Jimmy Carter went to Poland on an official visit. While there he spoke on Polish TV and radio to the Polish people. He began his presentation by saying that "I love the Polish people." Unfortunately, the person translating his speech did not have a direct translation for the English word "love" into a comparable Polish word. When he translated the word "love" into Polish, the translator said that President Carter ". . .wanted to make love to the Polish people." Obviously, there was a furor over the translation and an embarrassment for President Carter.

The same problem exists for translations from Hebrew and Aramaic to Greek and from all three languages to English. Some languages have only one word that has a particular meaning while others have several. Some languages have words that do not translate into other languages.

Bible scholars generally agree that Moses wrote the first five books of the Old Testament. There are several language issues that present themselves in those early books that require both knowledge of language and an understanding of the geography of the region. For instance, in Exodus it says:

> *The Israelites traveled from Rameses to Succoth, about 600,000 soldiers on foot, besides their families. An ethnically diverse crowd also went up with them, along with a huge number of livestock, both flocks and herds." (Exodus 12: 37)*

If we assume that there were 600,000 soldiers with the Israelites during their exodus from Egypt, besides their families, how many total soldiers and family members were in the exodus? Considering the number of women, children, and the aging, along with the "ethnically diverse crowd" mentioned in verse 37, just how many people were marching into the wilderness following Moses?

If we figure, conservatively, that each of the 600,000 fighting men had three additional dependents, that would mean that the number of people leaving Egypt would be at least 2.4 million. Then, consider that these people could have been marching in an orderly fashion with ten abreast and, perhaps six feet between the rows. (That is a real stretch of the reality of the situation considering the flocks and herds.) How long would the procession stretch? The answer is most likely more than 300 miles. Then, figure how long it would have taken for 2.4 million people to get across the Reed Sea if they were still traveling ten abreast in an orderly fashion. (The original scripture says "Reed Sea" not Red Sea.) A person can normally walk about ten miles a day. When the cowboys of the Old West were herding cows on a cattle drive, they normally expected to cover about six miles each day. So, how long would it take the Hebrew Nation procession, spread backward into the desert 300-plus miles, to cross the Reed Sea? It is reasonable for us to assume that it would have taken days for that many people to cross the sea as it was described in the scriptures.

In Exodus it tells us that Pharaoh chased the Israelites:

> *So he got his chariot ready and took his troops with him; he took 600 of his best chariots and all the rest of the chariots of Egypt, with officers in each one. . . The Egyptians, all Pharaoh's horses and chariots, his horsemen, and his army, chased after them . . . (Exodus 14:6, 9)*

Further, the scriptures tell us that the Israelites were:

. . . terrified and cried out to the Lord for help. (Exodus 14:10)

If the Israelites had 600,000 fighting men, why would they have been terrified of the 600 chariots in the lead force of Pharaoh's army?

In a later scripture, the Amalekites, a small band of nomads who lived in the Sinai desert, attacked the Israelites while they were encamped around a water hole on the Sinai. The desert region of the Sinai, with its limited resources, has never been able to support more than about 6,000 people. If, from that number of 6,000 Amalekites, we assume that 2,000 were fighting men, is it logical that the Amalekites would have attacked a force of more than 600,000 or that the Israelites would have had much difficulty dispatching the attackers with such a numerical advantage?

Forty years or about two generations later, after the Hebrew Nation had suffered through their exile in the wilderness, Joshua led them across the Jordan River into the Promised Land. The scriptures tell us about the crossing:

The Reubenites, Gadites, and half the tribe of Manasseh went in battle formation in front of the Israelites, as Moses had instructed them. About 40,000 equipped for war crossed to the plains of Jericho in the Lord's presence. (Joshua 4: 12-13)

That number of 40,000 soldiers might be an accurate number available to Joshua for the fight that was to come if the original number of fighting men with the Hebrew Nation leaving Egypt had been around 6,000 as opposed to the 600,000 number we find in the Book of Exodus.

Obviously, the original number listed in Exodus 12: 37 needs to be questioned. The English translation may have been made from the original Hebrew or from Greek. That information is not available. However, neither language uses the number "zero" and numbers like 600,000 could be 60,000 or 6,000 or even 6. In short, there is no way to know how many fighting men were available to the Israelites. A smaller number would make more sense for the rest of the scriptures that followed.

COMPARISON OF NUMBERS

Arabic	Greek	Roman	Hebrew
0			
1	α	I	א
2	β	II	ב
3	γ	III	ג
4	δ	IV	ד
5	ε	V	ה
6	ς	VI	ו
7	ζ	VII	ז
8	η	VIII	ח
9	θ	IX	ט
10	Δ	X	י

Note: Arabic is the only one that has a zero

Moses caused a census to be taken that is presented in the Book of Numbers. The total listed there for the twelve tribes was just over 600,000 fighting men. That is consistent with the number presented in the Book of Exodus. Moses, of course, gets credit for writing both the books of Exodus and Numbers. The Old Testament was translated into English from either the Hebrew or the Greek languages so there is good reason for the possible discrepancy between the numbers listed and the reality of the situation.

More to the point of the miraculous content of the scriptures, would it really make a difference how many fighting men were in the procession of the Hebrew Nation as it made its exodus from Egypt? Would the miracles that happened be less important or fail to show God's hand in the process if the numbers were smaller?

The examples above are intended to show that translation of language is key to our understanding of what was originally written and the message that was intended by God and by the writer He used to convey His message. This is why Christian seminaries teach Hebrew and Greek to ministerial students who are preparing to lead modern day churches and missionary efforts. From time to time, they need to go back to the original language to know what was written and what God intended without the ambiguity of translation from another language.

The fact that Alexander the Great required that all within his new empire use the Greek language was very important in the spread of the gospel when Paul the Apostle and the other missionaries began traveling throughout the Middle East. There were several languages used in the Holy Land at the time. Aramaic was the language of the street spoken by most throughout the Middle East. Hebrew was the language of the Jewish religion. The Roman language of that time was a cross between local tribal languages in Italy and what we refer today as Latin. Many had to learn the Roman language to get along with their rulers. All of these languages were used by specific groups and none were what you could call universal languages. By virtue of the conquests of Alexander the Great, Greek had become the universal language, the only language spoken by virtually all who lived in the region. The spread of the gospel would have been greatly inhibited if missionaries carrying the good news had not been able to converse freely with the people whenever they crossed over a province's border. Thus, the spread of the Greek language through the conquests of Alexander the Great was very important to the overall plan that was put in place when Jesus came to walk among His people.

THE DIFFICULTY OF TRAVEL DURING BIBLE TIMES

Much of the travel during Bible times was extremely dangerous. That was true as it related to the countries in the region. It was especially true during the Roman domination of the region. History makes much of the so-called *Pox Romani* or three hundred years of Roman Peace. Since Rome dominated the other powers throughout their empire, there were few wars between countries. That was not true, however, for normal people who were attempting to get from place to place or to trade with other merchants within a region. Journeys were hazardous and necessitated traveling with a caravan with enough fighting men to protect both the people and the merchandise.

The Roman method for governing their empire was important to how travel occurred or, indeed, who could travel freely from place to place. The Roman government desired both peace and taxes from their provinces. They believed that as long as they were able to keep the various provinces separate from each other, no single entity could rise against Roman rule. Thus, they made a concentrated effort to see there was no common language, religion, and trade necessities such as currency or weights and measures. They believed such restrictions would keep the various provinces within their empire from organizing together to revolt. In contrast, the approach to governance by Alexander the Great was not to separate the various countries but, instead, to unify the various peoples under his rule by promoting a common language, schools, libraries, and business practices. (Note the map of the Roman Provinces in the map section.)

During this period of history anyone with Roman citizenship could move freely from province to province. However, a non-citizen was not free to cross a border to enter another province. At times even Paul the Apostle, a Roman citizen, had some difficulty moving freely, as is noted by the scriptures:

> *They went through the region of Phrygia and Galatia and were prevented by the Holy Spirit from speaking the message in the province of Asia. When they came to Mysia, they tried to go into Bithynia, but the Spirit of Jesus did not allow them. So bypassing Mysia, they came down to Troas. (Acts 16: 6-8)*

It is not known how the Holy Spirit or the Spirit of Jesus influenced Paul and his group of missionaries not to enter the two provinces. However, it has always been usual for God to assert His will by using what was already in place either in nature or by man. It is easy to envision that the Roman border soldiers would not allow Paul and his group of missionaries to enter either of the provinces of Asia or Bithynia. God, obviously, wanted Paul to continue on into southern Europe with the gospel and so, after a short rest in Troas, the next stop of the group was across the Aegean Sea to Philippi of Macedonia.

Roads were built from one end of the Roman Empire to the other but the only merchants or military crossing borders on those roads were Roman. The local people were stuck within their own borders. Further, the rural areas outside of the cities were populated by outlaws wanted by the Romans so robberies and other lawless activities were common on the roads between cities even within the boundaries of a province. In addition, groups called Zealots, an anti-Roman faction of the Jews, were also active between the cities. Thus, travel was always hazardous. (Note that among Jesus' Apostles was one called Simon the Zealot. It is possible, even probable, that Judas Iscariot and Barabbas, who was freed at Jesus' trial, were also Zealots.) It was necessary to always travel with a group whenever you left your city even within the Holy Land. Note the scripture related to Jesus' first trip to Jerusalem when he was twelve and the reference to a "traveling party":

> *After those days were over, as they were returning, the boy Jesus stayed behind in Jerusalem, but His parents did not know it. Assuming He was in the traveling party, they went a day's journey. Then they began looking for Him. (Luke 2: 43-44)*

The freedom of travel that came with Roman citizenship was an issue in spreading the gospel of the New Covenant. One may assume that God chose Paul the Apostle for his role as a missionary partially because he was a Roman citizen and could travel wherever the spirit led him. The same was true with others. When Barnabas and Peter set out on their missionary journeys, both chose Mark the Gospel writer to accompany them. Neither Barnabas nor Peter was a Roman citizen, yet Peter is recorded in the Bible as traveling widely, even all the way to Rome. That raises the question about the citizenship of John, who became John-Mark, and then Mark in the scriptures. Was he, like Paul, a Roman citizen? Some scholars believe he was. (See the section in the Appendix related to Mark and his citizenship.) That would explain his being chosen as a traveling companion by the older, more experienced missionaries. As a Roman citizen he could exercise his rights to cross the province borders all the way from Judea to Rome. And, of course, if he was free to travel he could also bring along his servants and companions as he moved from province to province.

SUMMARY

No study discipline stands alone. No one can have a complete grasp of God's message from the scriptures without first understanding the history, geography, and language of the Holy Land. It is comforting to accept that God is the same, yesterday, today, and always. It is less comforting to know that man is changing day by day and the circumstances that challenge man are constantly changing as well. If nothing else is learned from the study of *The World As It Was When Jesus Came*, the reader should realize that neither scriptures nor history exist in a vacuum. Each provides a window through which we can view what words were spoken and actions taken by Jesus and the other participants in the gospel story. Without having an understanding of both history and scripture, our knowledge is limited. We must be diligent in our studies and constantly open to God's truths.

THE HISTORY OF THE PERIOD LEADING UP TO THE BIRTH OF CHRIST, 400 B.C. – 4 B.C.

We begin this narrative 400 years before the birth of Christ. We are traveling about 700 miles west of the Holy Land to the Greek peninsula, where this civilization was developing its distinctive culture. By 350 B.C., the Greek culture was in full flower, a time known as the Hellenic Period.

You may have seen the movie *Troy* that came out a few years ago. Troy was a real place located on the extreme western coast of present-day Turkey. It is just south of the Dardanelles, the narrow area at the upper end of the Aegean Sea that extends northward into the Black Sea. The story told in *Troy* is about a war between the Greeks and Trojans over Helen, a Greek woman who was "stolen" by a Trojan soldier. We do not know for sure if the story is true or if it is fiction that sprang from the mind of a Greek writer. What we do know is that the story of Helen of Troy and the Trojan horse was taken from the book *The Iliad and The Odyssey* which was written by the Greek epic poet Homer. The fictional movie account of this battle did not enlighten us much about the history of that conflict but it did let us look at how the people lived, dressed, their weapons, and how their cities were built. By providing those insights the movie served a good purpose.

On the Greek peninsula, the various cities including Athens, Sparta, Corinth, and Delphi developed a governmental organization that came to be called city-states. Each of the cities had its own separate heritage and history but they had a common language and many cultural commonalities as well. They rejected uniting under one government as Greeks, though they traded with each other and often cooperated in battle, especially to protect themselves from the hated Persians.

The Greek cities were very advanced for their time, having well-developed business and commerce, schools for children, libraries, and surrounding walls for protection. Our history books tell us of the city-state Athens where they had free elections for leadership positions. It was the first experiment in history of democracy at work. Oddly enough, their elections were exercises of voting *against* what they didn't want rather than *for* what they did. Thus, every vote counted against someone instead of for someone. Whoever had the least votes in an election was the winner.

At the same time the city-states on the more southern sections of the peninsula were developing, there was a different kind of culture developing to the north, a more rural and nomadic type of life style. At the northern edge of the Greek peninsula was the territory known as Macedonia and the people there did not have walled cities. Most of the population of this region lived in little villages and moved on a regular basis to follow the grass lands and water for their flocks.

PHILLIP OF MACEDONIA

In the year 353 B.C. in Macedonia, a young man named Phillip was planning a new political and military force. Like the Greek city-states, the people of Macedonia were often harassed by the Persians. Phillip's goal was to unite the people of Macedonia for mutual protection from their primary enemy, the Persians, who dominated the Middle East from their capital city Babylon on the Euphrates River in present-day Iraq. At the young age of 30, he found himself with a small kingdom and a fairly capable army, but he knew his small force was no match for the dominant Persians. (Note the map of Macedonia and the surrounding territories in the map section.)

The Persian army had developed into an invincible military force for that time in history. They used elephants at the center of their charge. They had many chariots, which were the guided missiles of that time, and they put cutting blades on the wheels of their chariots so they could drive them into the opposition and do maximum damage to enemy soldiers. This was a time in history when most weapons were made of wood or soft metals. The Persians had perfected making metal that was harder than any of the metals made by the other civilizations in the region. They "fired" the metal in a forge to increase its strength, thus making their spear tips and swords durable weapons that would not fail in battle.

Into the power vacuum on the Grecian peninsula came young Phillip of Macedonia with a plan that would accomplish two purposes. First, he intended to convince the many Greek city-states to join with him in a mutual pact of defense that could create an army that would have a chance of protecting them all from the Persians. His second objective was to use that army to gain control of the entire Greek peninsula and all of the city-states. In essence, he intended to bring the entire Greek peninsula together under his leadership.

All of the Greek city-states were wary of Phillip of Macedonia and were worried about what he was planning. He was perceived as a threat to their independence, and that perception turned out to be real. Philip first consolidated his power base in Macedonia by bringing the tribes together under his rule. Then he moved south to the Greek peninsula and captured the smaller city-states of Polidaea, Phdna, Methune and Thersaly. After a short respite he moved on south and faced off with the combined armies of Sparta, Athens and Corinth. At the Battle of Chaeronea, he dispatched them, effectively ending the independence of the Greek city-states. From this point on, Philip had control of all of Macedonia and the Greek peninsula.

The Greeks viewed anyone and any country outside of their "enlightened" environment as uneducated, uncivilized barbarians. Phillip was no barbarian by any definition we use today, but nevertheless the Athenians gave him the name Phillip the Barbarian. Unfortunately, that name has followed him throughout history.

By this time, Philip was in his late thirties. He had three wives, including the beautiful Olympias, who had given him a son whose name was Alexander. He was growing into a young man just as Philip solidified his hold on the Greek city-states. At just eighteen years of age, Alexander was given command of one of Phillip's military units and rode alongside his father into battle.

Years before, Olympias had prevailed on Phillip to find a tutor for young Alexander. As was the practice of that time, wealthy families did not send their children to school like we do now. Instead, they looked for someone who was educated enough to provide training for their offspring. Olympias persuaded Phillip to bring a sophisticated, well-educated teacher back to Macedonia to tutor Alexander. The person Phillip persuaded to come home with him—probably for a significant amount of money—was the genius Aristotle from Athens.

It is an amazing "happening" in history when a genius appears to change the face of society, whether it is in the field of art or music as in the case of Michelangelo and Mozart, in science as in the case of Aristotle or Galileo, or in all of these at once as in the case of Leonardo da Vinci. Athens, with a regional population of only around 120,000 people at that time, had the good fortune to produce three men with genius capabilities in a rather short period of history. These men were Socrates, Plato, and Aristotle.

Socrates and Plato were philosophers who were known as master teachers for the young people of Athens. Aristotle was also a philosopher but, additionally, he was a mathematician, scientist, and engineer. He would become very important to the future of his young charge, then known as Alexander of Macedonia, later as Alexander the Great.

Though Aristotle was not a supporter of war for acquiring land or territory, his teachings in engineering allowed young Alexander to envision the tools of war in a new way. It was during Alexander's conquests that catapults for attacking the walls of cities and large movable scaffolds for scaling walls were developed along with other implements of war. Despite his feelings about war, Aristotle became very important to the future of his young charge and through him to the spread of Greek language and culture in later years as Alexander set out to conquer the known world.

ALEXANDER THE GREAT

When Alexander was around nineteen years of age, his father was assassinated. There were rumors that Phillip's wife, Olympias, was responsible but no one knows for sure. Thus, Alexander became the ruler of Macedonia and the Greek peninsula with its many islands at a very young age, beginning a time in history (337 B.C. – 323 B.C.) that would change the world and create effects still felt today. Perhaps no personality in history had so much impact on the world in such a short period of time. Certainly, no man who died at such a young age— he was just thirty-three--ever found himself to be the most powerful person in the world, capable of changing history for all time.

Alexander began his tenure as ruler of the Greeks and Macedonians by studying the war tactics of the Persians. He knew that his destiny lay in not only protecting his Greek lands from the Persian leader Darius and his army, but by defeating him and permanently ending the threat of the always aggressive Persians.

With Aristotle at his side, he devised a plan that not only would defeat the Persians but would protect his country for the foreseeable future. This plan included four parts:

1. He would tax his people and, with the money generated, he would create a "professional" army. Armies of that period in history were citizen armies. Men would work the farm or the herd, come when the leader called to join arms with other villagers to fight the current threat and, when the war was over, return to their lives in the villages. Most armies of that time in history only trained and fought in the summer. Soldiers needed to be home to plant and harvest crops each spring and fall and winter weather was prohibitive. Alexander envisioned an army that trained twelve months a year and used the most modern weapons available.

2. With the help of Aristotle's genius in the field of science, Alexander developed war machines for attacking walled cities that could negate the well-developed walls that most major cities used for protection. The previous tactic for taking a walled city was simply to surround it and starve its inhabitants into submission. Waiting for capitulation because of starvation required more patience than Alexander, a young man in a hurry, could tolerate.

3. He would not only take on the Persians and other military powers in their own regions but he would occupy the territories taken. Previously, when a war was fought the winner would take plunder from the cities, including valuables and slaves, and would return home to share the new-found wealth with the citizens. The conquered territories were abandoned and allowed to recreate their cities and their local governance. Alexander intended to keep whatever he took and to incorporate the new territories into his empire.

4. Once the new country or territory had become a part of Alexander's empire, he established business rules that required a standard process, including a common currency, weights and measures, and rules for the conduct of business that would allow trade to flow easily between territories. The language to be used in business was Greek and, thus, schools were set up that taught the Greek language and culture. Libraries were created as well as universities for the study of such skills as medicine and engineering. Contrast Alexander's plan for incorporating all conquered territories into his kingdom as equal partners with earlier conquerors such as the Assyrians, Babylonians and Persians and with the Romans who followed Alexander's conquests in history.

When Alexander the Great began the military conquest of all of those areas east of Greece, he did not realize that he would be fighting for ten years and when he finished would be the conqueror of the entire known world. By the time he had completed this military campaign, he had incorporated into his kingdom the Persian Empire that consisted of present-day Turkey, Iraq, Iran, Israel, Syria, Lebanon, and Jordan, as well as Egypt, the most powerful country of the southern region. Also included were countries well to the east, among them present-day Pakistan, Afghanistan, and a portion of western India. It is said that when he had conquered all of these areas he cried because there were no more worlds to conquer. (Note the map of Alexander's Empire in the map section.)

Of significance to Christian history is the fact that Alexander needed ships not only to move his soldiers and materials from place to place across the Mediterranean but also for trade purposes. With that in mind, he created a port on the coast of present-day western Turkey for his fleet. That port was established at what became the Biblical city of Ephesus. Today, the map shows Ephesus as a city located inland about ten miles from the coast but when Alexander built his port Ephesus was a sea coast city located where a small river emptied into the Aegean Sea. Over the past two thousand years erosion has pulled sediment out of the mountains down the river to create more land between Ephesus and the coast. Thus, the sea coast city of Ephesus is now an inland city.

Of major significance to the history of the world was the fact that Greek civilization was the most advanced of the time. Alexander's conquests helped spread the Greek language and culture. He ordered buildings and entire cities to be based on the model of Greek architecture, and established services such as schools and libraries, including the greatest in the world then and for centuries after at Alexandria in Egypt. He also built universities for the study of medicine and engineering. One of those universities was established at Tarsus, home town of Paul the Apostle. Luke, author of one of the Gospels, lived nearby in the Syrian city of Antioch, and it is likely he received his training as a medical doctor in Tarsus.

After Alexander's occupation of this huge region of the known world, the Greek language and culture became the language of both education and business. Trade could now be carried on from Greece to India using the same language, currency and other business necessities. It is also the reason why the New Testament was written in Greek. Hebrew was the language of a small segment of the Middle Eastern population but because of Alexander's influence every educated person knew Greek.

At the age of thirty-three Alexander died (323 B.C.) somewhere between Greece and India, evidently on the way home after his campaign in India. When he died the lands he had conquered were divided between four of his generals. Before long there was squabbling among them and fights broke out between the various units. The spread of Greek culture came to a halt, and in just a few years most that Alexander had created disintegrated into oblivion.

There were many prophecies in the Bible but one, especially, seemed to speak to the empire established by Alexander. It is found in the eleventh chapter of Daniel, when Daniel is having a conversation with an angel sent to him in a vision. The angel is speaking:

I will tell you what is recorded in the book of truth. In the first year of Darius the Mede, I stood up to strengthen and protect him. Now I will tell you the truth. Three more kings will arise in Persia, and the fourth will be far richer than the others. By the power he gains through his riches, he will stir up everyone against the kingdom of Greece. Then a warrior king will arise: he will rule a vast realm and do whatever he wants. But as soon as he is established, his kingdom will be broken up and divided to the four winds of heaven, but not to his descendants; it will not be the same kingdom that he ruled, because his kingdom will be uprooted and will go to others besides them. (Daniel 11: 1 – 10)

True to history, there were four more kings in Persia following Darius the Mede, who succeeded Belshazzar in Babylon. Greece is mentioned in the prophecy and the warrior king mentioned could be assumed to be Alexander the Great, who did rule a vast realm, but almost as soon as it was established he died and his kingdom was "broken up and divided to the four winds." The four winds could refer to Alexander's four generals who inherited his kingdom. (Interpreting visions and prophecies from the Bible is never an exact science. Still, this one is very close to what happened, as are many others.)

Following Alexander's death and the breakup of his empire, circumstances for the people of the Middle East returned to their pre-Alexander state. It remained that way until 230 B.C. when expansionist urges began to be felt in Rome, 700 miles to the east.

The major benefit of Alexander's conquests was his legacy of a common language, schools, libraries, and the sharing of the Greek city-states' approach to governance, which included the first experiment with democracy.

Of significance to future Christian missionary work in the first century A.D. and beyond was the universal use of the Greek language. When Paul the Apostle, Peter, John, Mark and the other missionaries began carrying out the great commission of Matthew 28: 19-20, it was a major advantage to be able to communicate with most of the educated population using the Greek language

THE ROMANS

While Alexander and Greece were challenging the eastern world and spreading the Greek culture from Egypt to India, Rome was beginning to stir on the Italian peninsula. The period of the Roman conquest began in 230 B.C. and over the next 300 years Rome moved slowly but deliberately over the lands previously conquered by Alexander the Great and across the European continent as well. Three hundred years later, when their empire faltered, the Romans controlled much of the land in three continents, Europe, Asia, and Africa. The Roman Empire extended from England in the north of Europe to Egypt in Africa to India in the heart of Asia. (Note the map of the Roman Empire in the map section.)

The Roman conquest followed much of the pattern created by Alexander. The Romans used a professional army, the latest in military technology, and occupied all of the lands they conquered. Unlike Alexander they did not incorporate each of the conquered territories into their empire as equal partners. Their primary desire from each of the conquered territories was peace and taxes. In each of the lands conquered they placed a military dictator, but they also created a local administration which was headed by a local citizen who served as governor. The Romans allowed the annexed territories to govern themselves in everything except issues that related to keeping the peace and paying taxes. In each province they kept a Roman legion close by in case it was needed.

When the Romans began to conquer the territories from northern Europe to India, they divided the responsibilities between two sets of legions. One was known as the Eastern Legions and the other as the Western Legions. In 63 A.D. Julius Caesar was commander of the Western Legions with responsibilities for conquests in central and northern Europe. The Eastern Legions were commanded by a general named Gnaeus Pompeius Magnus Pompey. It was Pompey who came to the Holy Land in 63 B.C. and, with little resistance, took control. He then went on to Egypt and added that country to the Roman Empire as well.

One of the positive things about the Roman conquest was that the Romans generally adopted whatever custom or practice that belonged to their new provinces that was an improvement on what they had in Rome. Thus, when the Romans conquered the Greek peninsula, they adopted much that was good about the Greek culture. They were so enthralled with the education and knowledge of the Greeks that they took many of the best and brightest educated Greek citizens home to Rome with them to help educate their children. Thus, Greek art, music, and science found its way to Rome. Bringing the best of the Greek culture home to Rome was most likely the motivation for creation of what Romans called The Republic, ruled by an established senate with an elected leadership. This innovation lasted until Julius Caesar came home at the front of his Western Legions and won a power struggle with both Pompey and the leadership of the senate. He then declared himself to be emperor. Julius Caesar became so revered in Rome that all the emperors who followed him took the title of Caesar.

One other innovation established by Julius Caesar was that he declared himself to be a god, as did many of the leaders of Rome who followed him. This was a source of major conflict with the Jews and Christians over the next century and led to their persecution. Unique to that time in history was the fact that following Julius Caesar's death a comet appeared in the sky. A popular myth said the comet was his spirit traveling across the sky to take his place with the other gods. Roman coins minted during that time had the Emperor Caesar's face on the front and a comet on the back, reinforcing the myth of his status as a god.

Our history books tell us much more about Julius Caesar than about Pompey, though Pompey actually conquered more territory than Caesar. The reason for this imbalance of information is the fact that the territories conquered by Julius Caesar were France, Germany, and England. We in the United States derive much more of our history from these countries than we do from the Middle Eastern countries conquered by Pompey. Also, when there is a power struggle between two powerful men, it is the winner who writes the history.

Twenty years after Pompey took the lands of the Middle East, there was a revolt by the Persians in eastern Turkey and it extended the rule of the Persians into Galilee of the Holy Land. Eventually, Rome sent an army to put down the uprising and to re-occupy the area. However, the revolt occurred during a time when the Romans were preoccupied with a challenge in another part of their empire and so there was a lag in the time required for the Roman legions to appear. The Persians settled into Galilee for about eighteen months, and then the Roman Legions returned to re-take the land. This uprising and its outcome are keys to understanding another part of the Holy Land story that will continue in the following section, and that relates to Herod the Great.

As previously stated, the Roman plan for controlling its empire included establishing a local governor backed by a military dictator and a Roman legion. In the Holy Land the most famous of the Roman dictators was Pontius Pilate. The early Roman dictators created a palace at Caesarea by the Sea about sixty miles up the coast from Joppa, where present-day Tel Aviv is located, or about ninety miles from Jerusalem. The most famous of the local governors was Herod the Great, designated by the Roman Senate as King of Judea. His palace was located in Jerusalem.

HEROD THE GREAT

Much of what we know about Herod the Great comes to us from the Historian Titus Flavius Josephus who lived in the first century A.D., just after Herod's death.

Herod was a Moabite who had converted to Judaism at an early age when the Moab ruler Hyrcanus decreed that all of his subjects would become Jews. Because of his closeness to the Holy Land and the weakness of his country it probably was a prudent action to change the religion of his people in order to better relate to the stronger country to his north. Herod was also a Roman citizen because his father, Antipater, had been awarded citizenship for his service to Rome. Unfortunately, history does not tell us what service he performed for Rome.

Herod was reported to be "clever and quick-tempered, with a reputation for efficient and sometimes brutal action." Herod's father was a major advisor to King Hyrcanus. Because of his father's influence Herod was given administrative control of the rural province of Galilee at the very young age of twenty-five. After about ten years of controlling Galilee, the previously mentioned Persian revolt occurred and the Persian army invaded from the north and took the province of Galilee, forcing Herod to flee south toward Moab, his traditional homeland. Previously, Herod had created a palace/retreat at Masada close to both the Dead Sea and Moab. He took his family there and then began an odyssey that would shape the rest of his life and the history of the Holy Land.

Herod went first to Moab asking for money to create an army to retake his province of Galilee. The Moab leadership did not want to get involved and turned him down. He traveled on across the desert to Egypt which was then controlled by Cleopatra who had become queen just a few years before. Cleopatra invited him to join her army as a general and have sanctuary in Egypt for himself and his family. Normally that would have appealed to Herod but he had a greater vision of his future.

Many years earlier when General Pompey was conquering the Holy Land, he had a young general named Marc Antony who he sent into Galilee. Herod, always the master politician, arrived at the Roman camp one night bringing several wagon loads of food to the legions. Through that effort he made friends with Marc Antony, who continued to advance through the ranks of Rome's army until he replaced General Pompey as leader of the Eastern Legions.

Now, years later, Herod's plan was to book passage on a ship from Egypt to Rome to find his friend, Marc Antony, and with his assistance place his petition for help before the Roman Senate. As was obvious, the Romans had much to gain by helping Herod return to reclaim Galilee.

Herod found General Marc Antony in Rome. With his help, Herod's plan began to take on another dimension which was far greater than he had ever imagined. Marc Antony took Herod to the Roman Senate and declared him to be a friend of Rome who, along with his father, had provided valuable service in the past. Great speeches were made about Herod and his loyalty to Rome and a banquet was held in his honor. In the end, the Roman Senate voted to declare Herod to be King of all Judea, the only king ever so voted by the Roman Senate. When Herod departed Rome for Jerusalem he had the support of the Roman Senate and, more important, he had the support of Rome's Eastern Legions.

A sidelight of the conflict between Herod, his allies from Rome, and the Persian rebel group related to Herod's stronghold at Masada. Herod's family had been there since he left for Rome. While he was gone, the Persian army had located them and put the mountain-top fort under siege. Knowing of the jeopardy to his family, Herod brought his legions quickly though the Holy Land toward the Dead Sea and Masada.

Word came in advance that the Roman Legions were advancing toward Masada and many of the Persian soldiers deserted. When the two armies met on the battlefield the outmanned Persian army was no match for the seasoned Roman Legions. Before long Herod and the Roman Legions had dispatched the Persian rebel force and Herod was established as the King of Judea, the most powerful man in all of the Middle East.

Herod the Great ruled for more than thirty years and passed his position of control down to his son, Herod Antipas, and through him, to his grandson, Herod Agrippa. The Herod family, with the support of Rome, ruled in the Holy Land for more than eighty years.

Roman records tell us that Herod the Great died in 7 B.C. We believe that Jesus was born in 5 B.C. and that Herod the Great was still king at that time, or so the Book of Luke tells us. Of course, the Book of Luke was written around 50 years later (around 55 A.D.) and so there may have been some confusion in Luke's mind whether Herod the Great or Herod Antipas was king at the time. Luke was a meticulous writer, however, and he was not given to mistakes. If we need to trust someone's accuracy on this matter we choose to trust Luke's rather than the Roman historians.

SUMMARY

The Greek conquests led by Alexander the Great followed by the creation of the Roman Empire greatly affected the Holy Land and the creation and development of the early Christian church. Key in the influence of the "happenings" of the previous 400 years was the spread of the Greek culture and language. Also key was the establishment of a common weights and measures system, trade administration, and what was then called the *Pax Romana* or Roman Peace, which extended well into the second century after the birth of Christ. Because of this peace there could be movement between England in the far north of Europe to India in Asia and down to in the northeastern corner of Africa. Nothing like this had ever existed before.

The early Christian church took full advantage of the Roman Peace for its missionary work with the creation of churches from the Middle East to Rome and beyond.

THE RELIGIOUS SETTING IN JERUSALEM AND THE HOLY LAND WHEN JESUS CAME

When Jesus came to earth to dwell among men, he entered a country that was under the political control of a military force from Rome, a governing administration headed by Herod the Great, and a religious hierarchy that dominated the lives of the Jews. There was an outward appearance of peace, yet just below the surface within this oppressed society was major internal conflict.

The Romans were constantly afraid of the potential of an uprising, which did occur multiple times during their occupation of the Holy Land. As a result they ruled with a very heavy hand. Almost any violation of Roman authority was answered with strong military force. Individuals who came under Roman scrutiny faced slavery or death.

King Herod had active opposition. The Jewish people saw him as an outsider, a Moabite who was a nominal Jew who didn't observe the rituals of their religion. Roman taxation was heavy but Herod's taxes were even greater. Within the Jewish religious hierarchy there was a constant conflict between the dominant Pharisees and the more conservative Sadducees. Just at the edge of the conflict were the Essenes who attempted to stay out of the line of fire and who cooperated with the dominant forces in the country as little as possible.

The scriptures talk about "wars and rumors of wars" in the Holy Land. Those wars and rumors existed 2,000 years ago just as they do today. In the twenty-first century, the conflicts often erupt into "hot" war between countries. When Jesus came 2,000 years ago the primary conflicts were between various segments of the governmental administration and the religious units that were in constant competition for dominance in the lives of the people.

Isaiah the prophet may have said it best as he described the coming of the Messiah:

> *The people walking in darkness have seen a great light; on those living in the land of darkness, a light has dawned. . . For a child will be born for us, a son will be given to us, and the government will be on His shoulders. He will be named Wonderful Counselor, Mighty God, Eternal Father, Prince of Peace. . . He will reign on the throne of David and over his kingdom, to establish and sustain it with justice and righteousness from now on and forever. (Isaiah 9: 2, 6, 7)*

Considering these circumstances, is it any surprise that virtually everyone was looking forward to the coming of the promised Messiah, the one who would save them from the Romans and the constant internal conflicts that dominated their land and their lives? Is it any wonder that they gathered in groups by the hundreds and thousands to listen as Jesus taught them around the Sea of Galilee and on the steps of the Temple in Jerusalem? The prophecy from Isaiah promised freedom from oppression, from impossible taxation, from constant fear, and at the same time justice and righteousness forever into the future. That prophecy could stir their hearts and make their spirits soar. Is it any wonder they prayed daily for such deliverance and that every expectation for the future revolved around the coming of the promised Messiah?

THE PHARISEES

The Jewish religion in Jerusalem at the time of the coming of Christ had three divisions. These were the Pharisees, the Sadducees, and the Essenes.

Much of what we know of the philosophy of the three divisions and their history comes from Josephus, the historian, in his book titled *The Antiquities*. He was born into a Jewish family in Jerusalem, fought against the Romans in two uprisings and retired from the military after the 67-73 A.D. war. He served as a Roman translator and began writing the history of the time and the region in the mid-70s A.D. His history books, *The Antiquities* and *The Jewish Wars* were two of only three history books written about that period of time that were preserved for our use, outside of the Bible. Because of his books we know much more about Herod the Great and his family, as well as the Jewish uprising of 67-73, which ended with the destruction of the city of Jerusalem and Herod's Temple. It also provided us the story of Masada and the Roman siege of the mountaintop fortress.

Josephus writes that establishing a time line for the origin of the Pharisees is complicated. There is no record of their beginning, just that they were on the scene and had become a major power within the Jewish religion during Jesus' time in Israel. In one historian's writing they were cited as "those who seek after smooth things." Thus, the Pharisees were reproached for taking the smoother or easier way as per Jewish law.

The name "Pharisee" gives us no real insight into the beginnings or the beliefs of the group since the name means only "those who are separated." That definition is not different from our perspective of those called to the ministry in the twenty-first century in that they are judged to be "called" and "separated" for that service.

The Pharisaic sect was composed of priests, laymen, craftsmen, farmers, merchants, those from the city and the country, Judea and Galilee. In other words, they were made up of the middle classes. At the time Jesus came into his ministry in about 27 A.D., it is estimated there were approximately 6,000 Pharisees in their group. Josephus tells us that the Pharisees can be further defined as a body of Jews who "profess to be more righteous than the rest and to explain the laws more precisely." He also points out that they were skilled in politics, more so than the Sadducees and Essenes, which was a necessary skill in order for them to prosper in that complicated religious and governmental time.

Worthy of note is the fact that the Jews of that time were devoted to the Torah, the first five books of the Bible which were written by Moses. They did read the other books of the Old Testament for history but the Torah gave them the principles and laws they lived by. Later in their history the writings of the prophets and the more historical documents in the Old Testament such as First and Second Kings and First and Second Chronicles became more accepted as per the practices of the Pharisee branch of Judaism. One of the "truths" by which they lived, written at the time in *The Antiquities,* would sound familiar to us today: "What is hateful to yourself, do not to your fellow. That is the whole Torah. All the rest is commentary."

The Pharisee influence was strongest during the first century following the birth of Christ, during the reign of Herod Agrippa I. After 50 A.D. the Zealots gained strength and the influence of the Pharisees waned. The Zealots' strength culminated in the revolt of 67-73 A.D. which was put down by the Romans and resulted in the destruction of Jerusalem and the temple that had been built by Herod the Great.

Some Pharisees participated in the revolt but most withdrew until the fighting was over, with the idea of stepping in and exerting influence in the aftermath. As a result, the Pharisee sect survived the destruction of 73 A.D. while the Sadducees and Essenes did not. Not much is known about the Pharisees and Jewish history following 73 A.D. since we have historic records from two sources of the time before the revolt but no record following that time.

THE SADDUCEES

As with the Pharisees, the key information we have about the Sadducees came from Josephus and his book titled *The Antiquities.* Josephus was very much in sympathy with the perspective of the Pharisees and thus he gave a biased viewpoint that was often negative toward the Sadducees. The Sadducees believed that the Pharisees were way too liberal and too willing to try new approaches to their religion. Though both believed in the rules and laws in the Torah, the Sadducees took a stricter approach to those scriptures while the Pharisees appeared to be more flexible. Josephus's writings show the Sadducees as very much in opposition to Jesus when he came on the scene.

The name "Sadducee" came from the word *Saddikim* which meant "righteous ones." They preceded the Pharisees on the scene in Jerusalem and interpreted the scriptures more conservatively than the Pharisees. Most of the priests of the Sadducees were older and came from the upper classes in the city and surrounding area. As is often the case, those who are born and live in "privilege" often look down on the middle and lower classes of people. That was certainly true of what Josephus wrote about the Sadducees. From their perspective the Torah was the authority for their practice of the Jewish faith and they saw no way to avoid the rules and laws written there. That was especially true of the laws pertaining to the Sabbath. They interpreted the laws in the Torah very literally and believed that not to follow each one was a sin that required sacrifice for forgiveness.

The Sadducees were more inclined to go along with their Roman overlords and did not want to draw attention to themselves or to rock the boat of the governor and his administration. From their perspective they were governed by the scriptures in the Torah and everything going on outside the temple with the people was none of their affair. Other beliefs of the Sadducees included their denial of the existence of angels and demons. They rejected the idea of the immortality of the soul and did not believe in Hell or eternal rewards or punishment for the lives they were living here on earth.

The Sadducees believed in a theocratic state under the leadership of the High Priest. Anyone who believed in the coming of the Messiah or held hope for deliverance from their oppression by a benevolent God was seen as a direct threat to the existing social and political order. Thus, Jesus' teaching and his new perspective was a direct threat to the wealth, social standing, and political position of the Sadducees.

THE ESSENES

As is true with our knowledge of the Pharisees and Sadducees, our primary source of information on the Essenes comes from the writing of the historian Josephus. He mentions them briefly in *The Antiquities* and includes a more complete description of them in *The Jewish Wars* that was written just after the revolt of 67-73 A.D. Of special interest is the fact that Josephus actually lived with the Essenes for a time.

We cannot say for sure but it is possible that the Essenes existed for thousands of years, much longer than the Pharisees or Sadducees. It is not clear whether the sect Josephus lived with was the same that we have identified as living at Khirbet Qumran. That group should be thanked for preserving the Dead Sea Scrolls that have become the center of scholarly investigation in the Holy Land since their discovery in 1947.

As stated earlier the Essenes may have existed centuries before the other major sects of Jews in the Holy Land but, like the Sadducees, there is no record of their existence following the revolt of 73 A.D.

In comparing the Pharisees, Sadducees, and Essenes, the Pharisees would be more liberal, the Sadducees more conservative, and the Essenes would be would be well to the right of the Sadducees. The Essenes felt strongly enough about separating themselves that they withdrew from the cities and towns of Judea and Galilee and set up their own towns and societies in the uninhabited areas of the region. Their settlement at Khirbet Qumran has become famous with the archeological studies in recent years. It is located in the mountainous region south of Jericho and close to the Dead Sea.

The Essenes believed that a person could only become a Jew by birth. They rejected any pleasure as an evil and believed in the pursuit of conquest over passions. They believed that women were naturally lascivious and were persuaded that no woman could preserve her fidelity to one man. Thus, they did not believe in marriage in the same way that modern day Jews and Christians do. They did allow marriage but only for the necessity of child bearing and caring for children. They were despisers of riches and believed that no one of them should have more than another. All goods within the group belonged to all and everyone's possessions were intermingled with everyone else's possessions. If you were looking for a pure example of communal living, an Essenes community would make a good model.

As with the Sadducees, the Essenes believed in the laws and rules in the Torah. They believed that our bodies are corruptible but, unlike the Sadducees, they believed that the soul would live forever. They believed in a judgment some day and the soul living forever with God. The Essenes did not worship in a temple with a group but, instead, prayed and practiced their religion individually. Baptism was a central belief of the Essenes and John the Baptist may have been influenced by them since he ministered close to an Essene settlement north of the Dead Sea.

THE SAMARITANS

Though the Bible mentions the Samaritans several times, once again most of what we know of that exiled group comes from the writings of Josephus the historian. The Samaritans were a fourth major religious group in the Holy Land. They were looked down upon as idolaters by the Pharisees and the Sadducees but, obviously, not by Jesus. The evidence is in his ministry and his effort at reconciliation and healing.

The land occupied by the Samaritans was about sixty miles north of Jerusalem on the high plains west of the mountain ridge near the ancient city of Shechem. This was near the location where Abraham brought his family on direct instructions from God some six hundred years earlier. The Samaritans made their living by herding sheep and cattle and, to a lesser degree, farming.

The Samaritans were one group that remained in the Holy Land after the exile to Babylon. They intermarried with Gentiles, failed to teach their children Hebrew, and were different from the Jews in many aspects of their lives. They lived difficult lives partly due to the lack of natural resources in their section of the country. Also, the dominant group in the region, the Jews, were restricted by their leadership from associating with them. Thus, trading in the cities was not a part of their livelihood.

Jesus used the example of the Good Samaritan in one of his illustrations of how we should treat others. That story would have been a sensation to the Jews of that time since the very idea of a "good" Samaritan was foreign to the Pharisee-dominated Jewish group. The scriptures also report the fact that when Jesus healed the ten lepers, only the Samaritan returned to give thanks to Him. Travel through the land of the Samaritans as well as association with that group of people were both forbidden. Still, the Biblical story of the woman at the well occurred when Jesus and His disciples traveled through the land of the Samaritans and He stopped to minister to the woman and her entire community for a few days.

Jews did not accept others of mixed race or people who did not regard the center of their religion as their capital city of Jerusalem. They regarded the Samaritans as a hybrid race who accepted only the first five books of the Bible, those books written by Moses, as the soul of their religion. Thus, they were different from the Jews who envisioned their God as living in Jerusalem and their scriptures as including the writings of the prophets as well as King David and others.

Josephus wrote that the impressions of the Samaritans by the Pharisee leadership of the Jews was flawed. The Samaritans were mostly descendants of Ephraim and Manasseh, two of the leaders of the original Jewish tribes. Their priests were descendants of Aaron, the brother of Moses. The Samaritans felt very much wronged by their treatment from the Jewish majority. They believed that the Ark of the Covenant should have resided at Mt. Gerizim as designated by the writings of Moses. They believed the temple should have been erected there and they blamed the prophet Ezra for erecting the second temple beside the Judean capital of Jerusalem instead of where it should have been. (Ezra, the prophet, got a bad rap from the Samaritans since he had nothing to do with the decision to rebuild the Temple in Jerusalem.)

Whatever the real cause of the split between the Samaritans and the rest of the Jews, that small group of Jews were outcasts. All of the Jewish restrictions that applied to the Samaritans held true until Jesus approached them directly on His travels and began to win them to His New Covenant.

EXPECTATIONS FOR THE MESSIAH

The word "expectation" is not hard to define. It means that we are looking forward to something or anticipating an outcome. No outcome was more anticipated among the Jews than the coming of the Messiah. The belief in the Messiah was central to their religion from the earliest days. The Messiah was promised to come and deal with the very issues of life and death for the Hebrew Nation. Nothing could have been more important to the people. Nothing could have hit closer to the fabric of Jewish life.

The word "Messiah" appears in the Old Testament twenty-nine times, beginning as early as the writings of Moses. Each time it relates to the reigning king and not to a religious figure. When it began to appear in the literature of later Judaism it had a broader religious meaning. It means "anointed." Anointing with oil had a special significance because it symbolized the transition of the person to a sanctified status. To be anointed denotes a special relationship with God. The first king of Israel, Saul, was anointed, as was David who followed him. It was believed that when the king was anointed he was endowed with a divine spirit and filled with superhuman power and wisdom.

Always in scripture there was one to come who would make life better, would lead the people out of bondage or would make life more bearable. By the time the Hebrew Nation had been in existence for a thousand years, Isaiah and other prophets were constantly speaking and writing about the coming Messiah. This created anticipation among the people that a better time was coming and the one bringing that better time was coming directly from God.

The expectations for the Messiah were always there with the Hebrew Nation, from the time of Moses who had led them out of captivity, welded them into a nation, and performed numerous miracles in the process. Throughout their years of oppression under the yoke of the Assyrians, Egyptians, Babylonians, Persians, Greeks, and finally the Romans, they were constantly looking forward to the time when their Messiah would appear. Isaiah promised them in his writing in about 700 B.C. that the Messiah would come:

> For a child will be born for us, a son will be given to us, and the government will be on His shoulders. He will reign on the throne of David and over his kingdom, to establish and sustain it with justice and righteousness from now on and forever. (Isaiah 9: 6-7)

It was the phrases "the government will be on his shoulders" and he "will reign on the throne of David and over his kingdom" that created the significant expectations the people had for the coming Messiah. From the perspective of future generations it was impossible to assign any meaning for those words other than that a savior for the people was coming. They believed Isaiah was saying that the Messiah would assume the leadership of His people, would help them throw off the chains of the Romans, would live forever and reign over the Holy Land and protect them into the endless future.

When Jesus came speaking words that gave comfort to the oppressed and challenged those in control, when He could do miracles of all kinds and even the ultimate--challenging death--it was obvious to many that the Messiah had come.

When Jesus came the people were expecting a political, military type of Messiah who would deliver them from the oppression of Rome. Such a Messiah appealed to the nationalistic sentiments of liberation associated with Moses and the exodus. Many were expecting Jesus to begin organizing them into a revolutionary movement at any time. Even Jesus' Apostles who were with Him throughout his ministry and heard His words every day were not sure of His purpose for coming. They envisioned the Messiah of Isaiah's prophecy and either did not hear or did not believe Jesus when He said otherwise.

Zealots were known in Israel to be strongly anti-Roman and working toward whatever would rid the country of these oppressors. One apostle, Simon the Zealot, was so named and identified as one of these anti-Roman people. It was likely that Judas Iscariot was also a Zealot judging by the way he reacted to Jesus' words to the disciples during his last days before his capture, trial, and ultimate crucifixion. When Jesus told them He had come for a purpose other than to take the government on His shoulders, it confused the group and they were not sure what the ultimate outcome would be. At that point it appears Judas Iscariot became sufficiently disillusioned to betray Jesus to the Pharisees.

The level of confusion among the Apostles was such that several times there were discussions about just who Jesus was. For years there had been the belief that several of the prophets would rise from the dead and return to lead Israel. These thoughts were in the minds of the people as Jesus walked and taught among them. The disciples voiced these influences when Jesus asked them who they thought He was:

Jesus went out with His disciples to the village of Caesarea Philippi. And on the road He asked His disciples, "Who do people say that I am?" They answered Him, "John the Baptist; others, Elijah; still others, one of the prophets." "But you," He asked them again, "who do you say that I am?" Peter answered Him, "You are the Messiah!" (Mark 8:27-29)

What being the Messiah meant, however, still escaped the understanding of the group. Jesus told them:

"You know that the Passover takes place after two days, and the Son of Man will be handed over to be crucified." (Matthew 25:2)

Again, Jesus spoke to them about what was to come:

He was teaching His disciples and telling them, "The Son of Man is being betrayed into the hands of men. They will kill Him, and after He is killed, He will rise three days later." But they did not understand this statement, and were afraid to ask Him. (Mark 9: 31-32.)

Thus, Jesus told them directly that He must be killed and then He would rise again. When Jesus spoke those words to those He loved most dearly, they did not understand. Such was the strength of the belief among the Apostles and His other followers that Jesus had come to assume the role of a political Messiah, to free Israel from oppression and to reign in Jerusalem "on the throne of David" as Isaiah had prophesied 700 years before.

SUMMARY

When Jesus began His ministry in the Holy Land He found himself in constant friction with the leadership of one or another of the religious groups of that time. The Pharisees were the dominant religious group and held the key positions that were important to the Jews. Thus, it was the Pharisees who most often confronted Jesus and challenged His teachings. And, it was the Pharisees who had the most to lose if the people accepted the teachings of Jesus.

Herod the Great, his son and grandson were the ruling family during that period of history in Jerusalem. Their primary motivation seemed to be to keep the peace and to walk a wary line between the religious factions of the Jews and the ruling overlords from Rome.

In the end it was the Pharisees who plotted against Jesus, bribed Judas to betray Him, and instituted a series of courts where He was destined to be condemned. None of this was a surprise to Jesus who had known it all to be foreordained. It was, however, a major shock to Jesus' closest followers who believed in the prophecy from Isaiah that said "the government would be upon His shoulders." They expected Him to reign forever with "justice and righteousness." Thus, the expectations for Jesus became very important as His ministry on earth came to a close with the cross.

SECTION II

TELLING HIS STORY

INTRODUCTION TO THE NEW TESTAMENT

The story of the birth, life, death, and resurrection of Jesus has generated an influence on the world that is impossible to estimate. The moral, ethical, and legal foundations of western society are based on His life and teachings. The life of Jesus has provided moral examples for daily life, proverbs, and even hope as death approaches. The calendar of the year is organized around the celebration of crucial moments in His life. In spite of the great diversity that has divided Christian communities and denominations, the basic story of the life of Jesus has been shared by all. The New Testament is a story of salvation and hope that has made Christianity what it is today.

The early writers called the story of Jesus' life and the spread of His ministry the New Testament. Some debated whether it should be called, instead, the New Covenant. Whatever it is called, the words recorded in the twenty-seven books of the New Testament are, indeed, a New Covenant between God and His people. Virtually all Christians agree that Jesus is the Son of God who came to earth to live among man and to provide a living example for the world. In general, the story of the life of Jesus is told in the four books of the Gospels: Matthew, Mark, Luke, and John. The directions for living as Christians, developing God's church, and spreading the word are found in the following twenty-two books. The final book in the Bible,

Revelation, is the New Testament's book of prophecy, written by the Apostle John.

THE LIFE OF JESUS AS TOLD BY THE FOUR GOSPEL WRITERS

The word "gospel" is a translation of the Greek word *euangelion*, meaning "good news" or "proclamation." The Gospels were written by followers of Jesus to proclaim the news of Jesus as the Christ. They were written for both believers and non-believers, for both instruction and to lead people to a saving faith in Jesus Christ.

THE GOSPEL OF MATTHEW

Matthew linked his Gospel to the prophecies in the Old Testament to justify his contention that Jesus was the promised Messiah. He tells the story of Jesus from miracle to miracle. His effort to persuade the Jews that Jesus was, in fact, the long awaited Messiah provided some of the best justifications to become a follower of Jesus found anywhere in the Bible and to spread   the gospel, the good news, to all the world.

WHO?

Most scholars believe Matthew was the disciple originally known as Levi, the tax collector. When he joined Jesus' group either he or Jesus changed his name to Matthew, just as Saul became Paul, and Simon's name was changed to Peter by Jesus. It was usual in Biblical times for people to change their names when their lives or jobs radically changed. Thus, when Levi moved from despised tax collector to disciple of Jesus, he became Matthew.

WHAT?

Biblical scholars believe that Mark's writing preceded both Matthew's and Luke's. It was obvious that Matthew read Mark's Gospel before writing parts of his book. Matthew was not concerned with chronology or linking the life of Jesus with historical happenings, dates, or the Roman or Hebrew leadership. He focused instead on providing a colorful and descriptive narrative of the life and "happenings" of Jesus as He moved among the people.

There is evidence that Matthew originally wrote his Gospel in the Hebrew language for the Jews and then, perhaps later, translated it into Greek for a more general distribution.

WHEN?

Matthew's second writing of his Gospel, in the Greek language, was written after Mark's and about the time Luke was writing his. It is likely that the three Gospel writers were together at that time, perhaps at Ephesus, around 60-65 A.D. Of the four Gospels, Mark's Gospel was written first, followed closely by Matthew's and Luke's. The Gospel of John was written about twenty-five years later.

WHY?

Matthew wrote his Gospel originally for the Jews and his purpose, obviously, was to convince the Jews that Jesus was the long awaited Messiah. His effort to persuade the Jews provided some of the best justifications to become a follower of Jesus found anywhere in the Bible and to spread the Gospel, the good news, to the entire world.

WHERE?

No one knows for sure where Matthew was when he wrote his Gospel. The city of Ephesus in present-day western Turkey is a likely choice since there was known to be a collection of the followers of Jesus and Paul there from time to time. It is mostly educated speculation, but the Christian church of Ephesus, under the protection of the Christian Bishop Onesimus, was known for its protection and nurturing of missionary followers. It is known that most of the Christian leadership was at Ephesus in the 67-73 A.D. period of the last Roman invasion. It is logical to assume that many were on the scene there prior to that time as well.

COMMENTARY ON THE GOSPEL OF MATTHEW

NAMES. Family names such as Hopkins or Smith were not used in Bible times and people were often known by where they were from, such as Jesus of Nazareth or Paul of Tarsus. Sometimes locations gave people a bad name. When the disciple Nathanial was told that Jesus came from Nazareth the scriptures tell us that he asked,

"Can anything good come from Nazareth?" (John 1: 46)

Mary Magdalene, one of Jesus' close associates, was known as a reformed prostitute even though there is no evidence in the Bible anywhere to support that contention. She was from Magdala, a small town on the Sea of Galilee close to the Roman city of Tiberius. Magdala was a location where Romans were known to visit prostitutes. Thus, Mary was judged, perhaps erroneously, by where she was from and not by her actions in the scriptures.

THE SIMILARITY OF THE FIRST THREE GOSPELS. Mathew and Luke obviously used Mark's Gospel as a guide when they wrote theirs. Matthew repeated many of the stories and examples used by Mark, sometimes telling them differently, thus giving a different perspective to the "happening," but sometimes telling the story almost in the same words used by Mark. Note the scriptures where both Matthew (Matthew 9: 9-13) and Mark (Mark 2: 14-17) describe the calling of Matthew to become a disciple by Jesus. The same story is told in Luke (5:27-32) but it has more original wording.

NOTABLE WRITINGS. There are many notable writings in Matthew's Gospel. Chief among them are the Sermon on the Mount (Matthew 5: 1-10) that some judge to be a concise summary of the teachings of Jesus, and the Great Commission (Matthew 28: 19-20), where he directed his disciples to spread the gospel. These are both judged to be of great importance in the overall presentation of the gospel.

LANGUAGE. As was true of all the disciples, Matthew was multi-lingual. He would have spoken Aramaic, the language of the common people of the Holy Land; Greek, the language of the educated population of the region; and Hebrew, his religious language as a Jew. He would also have been able to speak Roman/Latin, the language of the conquerors for whom he worked as a tax collector. When Matthew wrote his Gospel he most likely wrote it first in Hebrew since he was writing primarily to the Jewish population. Later, most likely when he was in Ephesus, he wrote an updated version in Greek, which was the most universal language of the region during that period in history.

KEY SCRIPTURES FOR MATTHEW

Matthew was mentioned in four lists of the original twelve Disciples: Matthew 10:3, Mark 3:18, Luke 6:15, and Acts 1:13. He was also mentioned in Matthew, Mark, and Luke in the story of his call to be a disciple by Jesus. Note the similarity of the stories told by each of the writers.

And as Jesus passed on from there, He saw a man called Matthew, sitting in the tax office; and He said to him, "Follow Me!" And he rose, and followed Him.

And it happened that as He was reclining at the table in the house, behold many tax-gatherers and sinners came and were dining with Jesus and His disciples.

And when the Pharisees saw this, they said to His disciples, "Why is your Teacher eating with the tax-gatherers and sinners?"

But when He heard this, He said, "It is not those who are healthy who need a physician, but those who are sick.

But go and learn what this means. I desire compassion, and not sacrifice, for I did not come to call the righteous, but sinners." (Matthew 9: 9-13)

And as He passed by, He saw Levi the son of Alphaeus sitting in the tax office, and He said to him, "Follow Me!" And he rose and followed Him.

And it came about that He was reclining at the table in his house, and many tax-gatherers and sinners were dining with Jesus and His disciples; for there were many of them, and they were following Him.

And when the scribes of the Pharisees saw that He was eating with the sinners and tax-gatherers, they began saying to His disciples, "Why is He eating and drinking with tax-gatherers and sinners?"

And hearing this, Jesus said to them, "It is not those who are healthy who need a physician, but those who are sick; I did not come to call the righteous, but sinners." (Mark 2:14-17)

And after that He went out and noticed a tax-gatherer named Levi, sitting in the tax office, and He said to him "Follow Me."

And he left everything behind, and rose and began to follow Him.

And Levi gave a big reception for Him in his house; and there was a great crowd of tax-gatherers and other people who were reclining at the table with them.

And the Pharisees and their scribes began grumbling at His disciples, saying. "Why do you eat and drink with the tax-gatherers and sinners? And Jesus answered and said to them, "It is not those who are well who need a physician, but those who are sick.

I have not come to call the righteous but sinners to repentance." (Luke 5: 27-32)

MATTHEW: LINKING HIS BOOK TO THE OLD TESTAMENT PROPHESIES

In his writing, Matthew continually refers to passages from the Old Testament in order to link his words to the prophecies of men such as Jeremiah and Isaiah:

The people walking in darkness have seen a great light; on those living in the land of the shadow of death a light has dawned.

For to us a child is born, to us a son is given, and the government will be on his shoulders. And he will be called Wonderful Counselor, Mighty God, Everlasting Father, Prince of Peace. Of the increase of his government and peace there will be no end. He will reign on David's throne and over his kingdom, establishing and upholding it with justice and righteousness from that time on and forever. (Isaiah 9: 2, 6-7)

This is how the birth of Jesus Christ came about: his mother Mary was pledged to be married to Joseph, but before they came together, she was found to be with child through the Holy Spirit . . . All this took place to fulfill what the Lord has said through the prophet: "The virgin will be with child and will give birth to a son, and they will call him Immanuel, which means, "God with us." (Matthew 1: 18, 22)

. . . he asked them where the Christ was to be born. "In Bethlehem in Judea," they replied, "for this is what the prophet has written: "But you, Bethlehem, in the land of Judah, are by no means least among the rulers of Judah; for out of you will come a ruler who will be the shepherd of my people Israel." (Matthew 2: 4-7)

Then what was said through the prophet Jeremiah was fulfilled. . . (Matthew 2: 17)

A voice is heard in Ramah, weeping and great mourning, Rachel weeping for her children and refusing to be comforted, because they are no more. (Matthew 2: 18)

Leaving Nazareth, he went and lived in Capernaum, which was by the lake in the area of Zebulun and Naphtali—to fulfill what was said through the prophet Isaiah. (Matthew 4:13)

The people living in darkness have seen a great light; on those living in the land of the shadow of death a light has dawned. (Matthew 4:16)

A STORY TOLD NOWHERE ELSE IN THE BIBLE

Perhaps only Matthew, the former tax collector, would think this to be a significant story to share with the world about Jesus. Jesus did pay His tax but He found a unique way to provide the money.

After Jesus and his disciples arrived in Capernaum, the collectors of the two-drachma tax came to Peter and asked, "Doesn't your teacher pay the temple tax?"

"Yes, he does," he replied. When Peter came into the house, Jesus was the first to speak. "What do you think, Simon?" He asked. "From whom do the kings of the earth collect duty and taxes—from their own sons or from others?"

"From others," Peter answered. "Then the sons are exempt," Jesus said to him.

"But so that we may not offend them, go to the lake and throw out your line. Take the first fish you catch; open its mouth and you will find a four-drachma coin. Take it and give it to them for my tax and yours." (Matthew 17: 24-27)

THE GOSPEL OF MARK

MARK

Mark was the youngest of the eye witnesses to write a book for the New Testament. His book contains nothing concerning the birth or early life of Jesus. Instead, more than half of the Book of Mark is focused on the arrest, trial, crucifixion, and resurrection of Jesus. Mark, like Matthew, attempted to demonstrate the deity of Jesus by highlighting the miracles Jesus performed. He wrote his Gospel to the Gentiles, as opposed to the Jews, for the expressed purpose of proclaiming Jesus as the Son of God, the expected Messiah, and one completely in control of the physical as well as the spiritual environment.

WHO?

From the beginning, the Gospel of Mark has been identified as the work of John Mark, son of a woman named Mary, whose home was a meeting place for Christians in Jerusalem. Mark was always on the fringe of the story of Jesus as it unfolded in the various Gospels and later as the word was spread by Paul, Barnabas, Silas, Luke, and the rest of the missionaries who carried the Good News to the Middle East.

Mark is identified in the scriptures as a cousin of Barnabas, who was a Levite. Thus, it is likely that Mark was also from the tribe to whom Moses had delegated responsibility for the religious life of the Jews. Over and over Mark was identified as a companion of Peter as they traveled through the Middle East and all the way to Rome.

WHAT?

Mark's Gospel focuses on the actions of Jesus as opposed to what Jesus said. Most of the major sermons of Jesus do not appear in the Gospel of Mark. Because of Mark's relationship with Peter, his Gospel is believed to contain essentially the story of Jesus as told by Peter. He wrote his Gospel in the Greek language knowing that his audience was far wider than the Jews of the Holy Land.

WHEN?

It is likely that Mark's Gospel was written over a period of years but finished between 55 A.D. and 63 A.D., in time for it to be used as resource for both Matthew and Luke as they wrote their Gospels. All may have been together from time to time during the A.D. 33-73 period and all certainly were together in the late 60s and early 70s A.D. in Ephesus.

WHY?

Mark attempted to demonstrate the deity of Jesus by highlighting the miracles Jesus performed. He wrote his Gospel to the Gentiles, as opposed to the Jews, for the express purpose of proclaiming Jesus as the Son of God, the expected Messiah, and one completely in control of the physical environment as well as the spiritual.

WHERE?

No one knows for sure where Mark was when he wrote his Gospel, though speculation is that it was written in Rome while he was traveling there with Peter. Peter died in Rome and that event may have motivated Mark's writing. It is thought that following Peter's death he went from Rome back to the safe haven that Ephesus had become.

COMMENTARY ON THE GOSPEL OF MARK

Mark was from Jerusalem and was the son of a woman named Mary who, tradition tells us, lived just outside the west wall of the city. We do not know who Mark's father was, just that Mark lived there in Jerusalem with his mother. The family was Jewish and Mark was known by two names, John and Mark, or in some cases John-Mark. The name John is a Jewish name and Mark is Roman in origin. The fact that in the scriptures he was called John, then John-Mark, then Mark raises the speculation that, like Paul, he may have been a Roman citizen. There is other evidence of Roman citizenship that will be cited later.

According to tradition, the house where Mark and his mother lived was a big house with two floors and a court yard with a wall and a gate. Some speculate that it may be the house where the last supper was held but no one knows for sure. We know it is a large house because Peter once came to the gate late at night and asked for entry. A servant girl heard his call and went to see who it was. She then went back inside to report Peter's arrival and ask permission to allow him to enter.

We know that Peter and the disciples must have come there often because the disciples were gathered there for prayer the night Peter arrived after being freed from jail. Peter knew where to come and he had been there often enough that the servant girl knew his voice in the dark.

At that point in time Mark was probably only thirteen or fourteen years of age. He would have been helping his mother serve the disciples. A Jewish boy at that age is on the brink of adulthood. From an educational perspective he has been taught by his mother the skills of reading, writing, and arithmetic. At around twelve years of age it was normal for the male child to begin accompanying his father to the work place. The scriptures do not mention that Mark had a father on the scene. His mother Mary may have been a widow.

Jewish tradition says that if a man dies and leaves a widow, especially one with children, the family designates another man in the family to take care of her. If the man who died has a brother, then the brother is to marry the widow. If not, then another male may be designated for the care responsibility. This may explain the presence of Barnabas in Jerusalem. He was a native of Cyprus but, obviously, was living close by Mary and her teenaged son, Mark. He also takes an active part in the parenting and development of Mark as is illustrated by his desire to have the boy along on the early missionary trips with Paul.

In serving the disciples, Mark would have had opportunities to come to know them and to hear much of what they said, though his level of understanding may have been limited. It is obvious in Mark's Gospel that he is impressed by Jesus and all of his close followers. Their influence appears over and over in Mark's missionary work and in his later writings.

Like Matthew, Mark was able to speak several languages. Hebrew was from his Jewish tradition in Jerusalem, Aramaic was the regional language of the street, Greek was spoken by all who were educated, and an early form of Latin was the language of the Roman conquerors. One of the clues as to where this Gospel was written was in the language of its writing. Items of interest to the Jews, such as the genealogy of Christ, fulfilled prophecy, references to the law, etc., were omitted. Mark used a number of Aramaic and Latin terms/words in place of their Greek equivalents. This raised speculation that the Gospel, written largely in the Greek language, was written in Rome and, perhaps, directed to the Romans.

As stated earlier, Mark was close to Barnabas, his cousin, and by virtue of that relationship was brought into the mission effort early. He was included on the first mission journey of Paul and Barnabas, which included stops in Antioch, Cyprus, and several cities in present-day Turkey. Mark left this journey and returned to Jerusalem, though the scriptures do not tell us why. It is speculated that he may have become homesick or was concerned about his widowed mother. Paul was upset with Mark for leaving them and this created a breach in the friendship of Paul and Barnabas. It was several years before the relationship between Paul and Mark was mended. Late in Paul's ministry it was obvious that Paul and Mark were again working and traveling together so it seems they re-kindled their relationship and Mark rejoined Paul's missionary efforts.

In his Gospel, Mark focused on actions as opposed to words. He included descriptions of eighteen of Jesus' thirty-five miracles but only two of his many sermons. His vivid descriptions are more detailed than the ones contained in Matthew and Luke and he uses a wide range of emotional reactions such as:

"They were amazed" (Mark 1: 27); "They feared exceedingly" (Mark 4: 41); "They laughed Him to scorn" (Mark 5:40); "They were offended at Him" (Mark 6: 3); and "They were astonished beyond measure" (Mark 7: 37).

Unlike Matthew and Luke, Mark passed completely over the events leading up to the birth of Jesus and His early life. He started his narrative just before Jesus began his public ministry.

More than a third of the Gospel of Mark is devoted to the events leading up to the trial of Jesus, His death and resurrection, and the effects of these events on the disciples. It is understandable that a young man watching events from the edge of the circle around Jesus would focus on the things he observed. The birth of Jesus predated Mark's birth. The trial and crucifixion, on the other hand, would have made a major impact on a young man and this event shaped the rest of Mark's life.

KEY SCRIPTURES FOR THE GOSPEL OF MARK

About the home of John-Mark and his mother, Mary:

> And when Peter came to himself, he said, "Now I know for sure that the Lord has sent forth His angel and rescued me from the hand of Herod and from all that the Jewish people were expecting." (Acts 12:11)

> And when he realized this, he went to the house of Mary, the mother of John who was also called Mark, where many were gathered together and were praying. (Acts 12:12)

John-Mark and his mother are most likely a part of the tribe of Levi. Barnabas, a cousin, is identified in the scriptures as being a Levite:

> Aristarchus, my fellow prisoner, sends you his greetings; and also Barnabas' cousin Mark, about whom you received instructions: If he comes to you, welcome him. (Colossians 4:10)

> And Joseph, a Levite of Cyprian birth, who was also called Barnabas by the apostles, which translated means, son of encouragement. (Acts 4:36)

John-Mark may have identified himself as the young man written about in Mark 14: 51-52:

> And a certain young man was following Him, wearing nothing but a linen sheet over his naked body; and they seized him. But he left the linen sheet behind, and escaped naked.

John-Mark traveled with Paul and Barnabas on the first missionary journey:

> And Barnabas and Saul returned from Jerusalem when they had fulfilled their mission, taking along with them John, who was also called Mark. (Acts 12:25)

> Now Paul and his companions put out to sea from Pamphylia; and John left them and returned to Jerusalem. (Acts 13:13)

Paul was upset enough at Mark having left them on the earlier journey that when Barnabas wanted to take him along on the later journey Paul refused to take him. This created a disagreement between Paul and Barnabas and the two split and went in different directions:

And after some days Paul said to Barnabas, "Let us return and visit the brethren in every city in which we proclaimed the word of the Lord, and see how they are."

And Barnabas was desirous of taking John, called Mark, along with them also.

But Paul kept insisting that they should not take him along who had deserted them in Pamphylia and had not gone with them to the work.

And there arose such a sharp disagreement that they separated from one another, and Barnabas took Mark with him and sailed away to Cyprus.

But Paul chose Silas and departed, being committed by the brethren to the grace of the Lord.

And he was traveling through Syria and Cilicia, strengthening the churches. (Acts 15: 36-39)

John-Mark is identified as a constant companion of Peter:

Through Silvanus, our faithful brother for so I regard him, I have written to you briefly, exhorting and testifying that this is the true grace of God. Stand firm in it. She who is in Babylon, chosen together with you, sends you greetings, and so does my son Mark. Greet one another with a kiss of love. (1 Peter 5:12-13)

Mark's Gospel is believed to contain essentially the story of Jesus as told by Peter. The emphasis within the text of the scriptures is of Jesus the servant. The essence of Mark's Gospel is contained in the following verse:

Yet it shall not be so among you; but whoever desires to become great among you shall be your servant. And whoever of you desires to be first shall be slave of all. For even the Son of man did not come to be served, but to serve, and to give His life a ransom for many. (Mark 10:43-45)

And when he had called the people to Him, with His disciples also, He said, to them "Whoever desires to come after Me, let him deny himself, and take up his cross, and follow Me. For whoever desires to save his life will lose it, but whoever loses his life for My sake and the gospel's will save it. For what will it profit a man if he gains the whole world, and loses his own soul? Or what will a man give in exchange for his soul?" (Mark 8: 34-37)

The Gospel of Mark is a book that shares the life of Jesus in a very matter-of-fact approach focusing on the "happenings" as a young man would, with wonder and strong impressions. That is especially true in the section of this Gospel that deals with the arrest of Jesus in the Garden of Gethsemane. The following is a story told nowhere else in the Bible:

Just as he was speaking, Judas, one of the Twelve, appeared. With him was a crowd armed with swords and clubs, sent from the chief priests, the teachers of the law, and the elders. Now the betrayer had arranged a signal with them: "The one I kiss is the man; arrest and lead Him away under guard." Going at once to Jesus, Judas said, "Rabbi!" and kissed Him. The men seized Jesus and arrested Him. Then one of those standing near drew his sword and struck the servant of the high priest, cutting off his ear. "Am I leading a rebellion," said Jesus, "that you have come out with swords and clubs to capture Me? Every day I was with you, teaching in the temple courts, and you did not arrest Me. But the Scriptures must be fulfilled." Then everyone deserted Him and fled. A young man, wearing nothing but a linen garment, was following Jesus. When they seized him, he fled naked, leaving his garment behind. (Mark 14: 43-52)

Most Biblical scholars believe that the young man in the linen garment is Mark. He is the only young man who was close to Jesus and the disciples during these events and certainly the only one who would have been in the Garden of Gethsemane on this fateful evening. If it was not Mark, how would he know about the incident?

THE GOSPEL OF LUKE

Luke was the only writer of a Gospel who was not a direct eye-witness to the life of Jesus. He gathered his story of Jesus by interviewing others who had close associations with the Messiah. At the beginning of his Gospel, Luke tells us his purpose in writing it. Luke wanted an accurate, chronological, and comprehensive account of the life of Jesus to strengthen the faith of believers and to help win the lost. He may have had a second purpose as well, to show that Christians were not a politically subversive group.

WHO?

Luke was born and raised in the city of Antioch, though we do not know if it was Antioch of Syria or Antioch of Asia (central Turkey). He was a physician. It is logical to assume that Luke studied medicine at a university in Tarsus, which was the closest university to his home city. It may also be logical to speculate that Luke may have met a young Saul (Paul) in Tarsus. Luke was the constant companion of Paul during the latter part of his life and became a fellow worker with Barnabas, Silas, Timothy, and Mark. Luke was most likely a Gentile as Paul made references to him that indicated he was not a Jew (Colossians 4:10-14). It is obvious from many things that Luke wrote that he may have been a Hellenistic Jew (a Jew by persuasion and not by birth and genealogy) though he was not a Hebrew Jew.

WHAT?

The Gospel of Luke is the most organized of the four Gospels, with dates and citations that allow us to place the happenings in history and location better than in the other Gospels. This is also the longest of the Gospels, and it is written with events in chronological order so that the story of Jesus can be followed day by day, event by event. It is logical to assume that Luke, not a personal observer of the ministry of Jesus, attempted to get multiple eye-witness accounts of events before he wrote them in his Gospel. He was particularly careful to give importance to the contributions of women in his writing and it is obvious that one of the people he interviewed was Mary, the mother of Jesus.

WHEN?

The date of writing was between 60 A.D. and 70 A.D., depending on what one believes about the chronology of events related to Paul's various captivities. Luke had access to Mark's Gospel before writing his, so it had to be written after 60 A.D.

WHY?

At the beginning Luke tells us his purpose in writing this Gospel. He says,

"to write to you an orderly account, that you may know the certainty of those things in which you were instructed." (Luke 1: 3)

Luke was concerned that Christians were often thought to be a politically subversive group. There is evidence in his writing that he hopes to ease those thoughts through what he wrote about Jesus and the new Christians. Note that he records Pilate's acknowledgment of Christ's innocence three times (Luke 23: 4, 14, & 22).

WHERE?

This Gospel could have been written at Caesarea by the Sea while Paul was in prison there or, perhaps, while Paul was under house arrest in Rome. He may also have written at least part of it after returning to Ephesus following Paul's death.

COMMENTARY ON THE GOSPEL OF LUKE

As stated earlier, Luke is assumed to be a Gentile from Antioch in either central Turkey or northern Syria. However, it is likely that he moved to Philippi or Thessalonica in Macedonia following his training as a doctor, which most likely occurred at the medical university in Tarsus.

The scripture tells us that Luke linked up with Paul in Macedonia during Paul's second missionary journey. This is the trip where Paul was stuck at Troas when he was intending to go to Bithynia up by the Black Sea. One night he had a vision of a man from Macedonia saying, *"Come on to Macedonia, we need you here" (Acts 16: 9-10).*

In the Book of Acts, Luke told the story of Paul and his travels through the second missionary journey. In Troas he begin using the pronoun "we" in his writings indicating he had joined the group. The word "we" continued to be used after Troas through the visits to Philippi and Thessalonica. When Paul left Thessalonica Luke did not use the word "we" again indicating he was no longer with the group. So, when Paul and his small band of followers took a boat from Troas across the Aegean Sea to the southern coast of Macedonia and then journeyed up to Philippi, Luke was with them. Luke was not mentioned prior to the stay at Troas so one could assume that he was not in the group until they arrived at Troas. It is then easy to assume that he was living somewhere in the area involved in his medical practice and then became the group's guide as they went into southern Macedonia. One continuing mystery is how Paul would have communicated with Luke to tell him where he was during his travels and where Luke could meet the group.

Luke stayed with Paul and the group at Philippi and Thessalonica during Paul's second missionary journey but did not continue with him for the rest of the journey. This gives credence to the contention that Luke was then a resident of that region and that he most likely had responsibilities there. If, as has been conjectured, Paul and Luke knew each other previously when both were young men in Tarsus while Luke was going to school there, it might account for both the communications between Paul and Luke and the obvious relationship between the two when they met in Troas. On Paul's third missionary journey he also traveled to that region of southern Macedonia where Luke was again with him. This time Luke evidently traveled with him from Philippi through the rest of this journey, through the fourth journey to Rome, and became his constant companion for the rest of Paul's life.

Bible scholars dwell on the belief that Luke was a Gentile, or a non-Jew. That would make him the only non-Jewish contributor to the writings in the Bible. There are those who contend that Luke was a Hellenistic Jew, a Jew who was not genetically of the Hebrew people from the Holy Land but who was a practicing Jew in Antioch through the early part of his life. The evidence of his being a Gentile was primarily from Paul's letter to the Colossians where Luke was grouped with the "uncircumcised" that were traveling with Paul (Col. 4: 12-14). Ordinarily, that would have meant that he was not a Jew. However, it is possible that Jews in places outside of the Holy Land may not have strictly followed the custom of circumcising their male children. (Until we can ask Luke about this face-to-face, we will assume along with most Biblical scholars that he was a Gentile!)

Luke was one of the great contributors to the Gospel of Jesus Christ. He wrote the books of both Luke and Acts which, together, are the longest and most comprehensive contributions to the New Testament by any single writer. Luke also was one of the scribes who helped Paul with his letters to the early Christian churches. Thus, he had the benefit of both information and instruction from Paul that may have made him the most knowledgeable of all the followers of Christ as the Bible was coming together later in the first century A.D.

The Gospel of Luke was written in Greek for a Gentile audience. Luke was the most educated of a well-educated group of men. In comparison to others of that place and time, the gospel missionaries were a talented group who planned and executed their great commission charge from Jesus in the latter part of the first century. Like most of Christ's early followers, Luke obviously spoke at least four languages. In addition, he most likely spoke Persian as well, which would have been the regional language of Antioch in either Syria or Asia. Luke was on hand with Paul during his imprisonment at Caesarea by the Sea and, later, in Rome. He served as a link to the churches that sent messengers back and forth to Paul while he was incarcerated.

To be in imprisoned in Bible times was very different from today. You had no promise of food, clothing, or legal help of any kind. You were judged to be guilty of the crimes for which you were charged. Jail was a place where you waited for either slavery or death. If you did not have friends on the outside to bring you food and to see to your daily needs, you could starve or freeze while you awaited your fate. Thus, Luke and others were life savers for Paul during his long periods in prison: two years and more in Caesarea by the Sea, two years under house arrest in Rome, and an undetermined time in Philippi and elsewhere. Paul spent lots of time in jail because the officials of that time did not know what to do with this citizen of Rome. Citizens of Rome could be dealt with only by the Roman leadership and not by the local governors appointed by Rome.

Luke may have been a strong influence on Paul in turning the emphasis for missionary work from the unsuccessful effort with the Jews to a much more successful effort with the Gentiles.

KEY SCRIPTURES FROM LUKE

Luke's name was mentioned only three times in the New Testament and all three passages mention Mark as well, indicating that Mark and Luke probably traveled and worked together:

Aristarchus, my fellow prisoner, sends you his greetings: and also Barnabas' cousin Mark about whom you received instructions; if he comes to you, welcome him… Luke, the beloved physician, sends you his greetings, and also Damas. (Colossians 4: 10, 14)

Epaphras, my fellow prisoner in Christ Jesus, greets you, as do Mark, Aristarchus, Demas, Luke, my fellow workers. (Philemon 1:23-24)

Only Luke is with me. Pick up Mark and bring him with you, for he is useful to me for service. (Timothy 4:11)

THE GOSPEL OF JOHN

As John was writing his Gospel he selected the signs he used with the purpose of creating intellectual *("that you may believe")* and spiritual *("that believing you may have life")* conviction about the Son of God. A key to much of what he writes is the word *"believe,"* and it requires that the reader have both knowledge and take action on that knowledge. The first three Gospels, Mathew, Mark, and Luke all tell of the life of Jesus and have much in common. John, the fourth Gospel, is very different in content and approach. It continually answers the question, "But why?"

WHO?

John and his brother James were the sons of Zebedee and Salome. The entire family was a part of the Christian movement almost from the beginning and both John and Salome were present at the crucifixion. It is speculated that Salome was a sister of Mary, the mother of Jesus, and, if so, that meant John was a cousin of Jesus. As a cousin he would have known Jesus all of his life and they were probably about the same age. John was evidently a follower of John the Baptist until he was called to follow Jesus at the beginning of His ministry. No disciple of Jesus was more influential while Jesus lived and following His ascension.

WHAT?

John's book is the most "different" of the four Gospels. He writes about events and discourses not found in the other Gospels to point out that Jesus is God in the flesh. John was probably writing primarily to the Greeks and because of this target audience much of his writing is more philosophical in its approach:

"In the beginning was the word, and the word was with God, and the word was God" (John 1:1).

The Greeks were known to be well educated and more philosophical in their approach to "thought" problems, which becoming a Christian certainly was. John wrote his Gospel not so much to tell what Jesus said but, instead, to tell what Jesus *meant* by what He said.

WHEN?

John's book was the last of the Gospels written. The dates would have been after 70 A.D. but, perhaps, before 90 A.D. By this point in time John would have been a man in his 80s and he would have been one of the last surviving eye-witnesses to the life of Jesus.

WHY?

John tells us clearly why he wrote his Gospel.

"But these are written that you may believe that Jesus Christ is the son of God, and that believing you may have life in His name" (John 20:31).

In writing his Gospel John selected the signs he used with the purpose of creating intellectual *("that you may believe")* and spiritual *("that believing you may have life")* conviction about the Son of God. The key word in much of what he writes is the word "believe," and it requires that the reader have both knowledge and take action on that knowledge.

WHERE?

John most likely wrote his Gospel in Ephesus sometime after 80 A.D. He spent the previous twenty years in exile by the Romans on the small island of Patmos in the Aegean Sea.

COMMENTARY ON THE GOSPEL OF JOHN

All of the disciples were well educated for their time and place in history but John was the closest to being an intellectual. In Acts 4:13 John is referred to as "uneducated" by the Jewish Temple leadership. He wasn't educated the way they were but he was, nevertheless, a very deep thinker. His writings provide some of the most thought-provoking scripture verses in the entire Bible. He introduces several of the staples of today's Christianity that must have been virtually impossible for people to understand during that time. Chief among these are the following:

"In the beginning was the word. . ." (John: 1); "For God so loved the world. . ." (John 3:16); ". . .who were born, not of blood, nor of the will of the flesh, nor of the will of man, but of God" (John 20:30-31); "I am the bread of life" (John 6:35); "I am the resurrection, and the life. . ." (John 11: 25).

If Jesus and John were cousins as some Bible scholars think, then it clears up a number of questions that are unanswered in the scriptures. Why was he so ready to go with Jesus when invited? Why, unlike Peter, the other leader of the disciples, was he so steadfast in his support and presence with Jesus? Five times in the scripture he was referred to as "the one whom Jesus loved." At the Crucifixion it was John to whom Jesus gave over care of His mother. It seems clear that John occupied a special place in the heart of Jesus and John's regard and unwavering support existed for more than fifty years after Jesus went back "to His Father's house."

John did not appear to be the perfect choice for a disciple at the time he was called by Jesus. He was known to have a temper and to hold a grudge. He, along with James, also had considerable ambition, as is shown in the effort of his mother to place James and John at Jesus' right and left hand *"when you come into your kingdom" (Mark: 10: 35-45).* In short, he was a normal man with a liberal amount of both strengths and weaknesses, just the kind of man that Jesus used to serve His ministry. Still, he conquered his weaknesses and Jesus used him mightily in the spreading of His Gospel.

Perhaps no other person in the Bible was so "present" in the scriptures as John. He was first a follower of John the Baptist, then followed Jesus when He came to the Jordan River to be baptized. Later, he joined Jesus at the beginning of His ministry. From that point on he was at every event, involved in almost every happening, supporting Jesus in every aspect of His public life. John was present at Jesus' trial, at the

Crucifixion, at the burial, just after the Resurrection, at the Ascension, and then continued to spread the word for the rest of his life. He wrote five books of the New Testament, four that bore his name. He most likely died in Ephesus in his late 80s or early 90s after writing Revelation. He was there in the company of the younger followers and supporters of Jesus under the protection of the Church of Ephesus.

KEY SCRIPTURES RELATED TO JOHN IN THE OTHER GOSPELS

And going on from there He saw two other brothers, James the son of Zebedee,

and John, his brother, in the boat with Zebedee their father, mending their nets;

and He called them. And they immediately left the boat and their father, and followed Him. (Matthew 4:21-22)

And many women were there looking on from a distance, who had followed

Jesus from Galilee, ministering to Him. Among whom was Mary Magdalene, along with Mary the mother of James and Joseph, and the mother of the sons of Zebedee. (Matthew 27: 55-56.)

And there were also some women looking on from a distance, among whom were

Mary Magdalene, and Mary the mother of James the Less, and Joses, and Salome. (Mark 15:40)

And he was going along by the Sea of Galilee, He saw Simon and Andrew, the brother of Simon, casting a net in the sea; for they were fishermen.

And Jesus said to them, "Follow Me, and I will make you become fishers of men."

And they immediately left the nets and followed Him.

And going on a little farther, He saw James the son of Zebedee, and John, his brother, who were also in the boat mending the nets.

And immediately He called them; and they left their father Zebedee in the boat with the hired servants, and went away to follow Him. (Mark 1: 16-20)

KEY SCRIPTURES FROM THE BOOK OF JOHN

When Jesus therefore saw His mother, and the disciple whom He loved standing nearby, He said to His mother, "Woman, behold, your son!"

Then He said to the disciple, "Behold, your mother!" And from that hour the disciple took her into his own household. (John 19: 26-27)

And Simon Peter was following Jesus, and so was another disciple. Now that disciple was known to the high priest, and entered with Jesus into the court of the high priest. (John 18:15)

I glorified thee on earth, having accomplished the work which thou gavest me to do; and now, gather, glorify thou me in thy own presence with the glory which I had with thee before the world was made. (John 17:4-5)

The light shines in the darkness and the darkness has not overcome it. There was a man sent from God, whose name was John. He came for testimony, to bear witness to the light, that all might believe through him. He was not the light, but came to bear witness to the light. (John 1: 4-8)

Again Jesus spoke to them, saying, "I am the light of the world; he who follows me will not walk in darkness, but will have the light of life." (John 8:12)

I have come as light into the world, that whoever believes in me may not remain in darkness. (John 12:46)

Behold, the Lamb of God who takes away the sin of the world. (John 1:29)

SECTION III

SPREADING THE WORD

In the aftermath of Jesus' time on earth the disciples organized to carry out the responsibility given them by Jesus to spread the gospel to all the world. There is evidence that they set out in different directions to do as Jesus commanded in Matthew 28: 19-20. They were joined in their efforts by a number of supporters and some, such as Paul the Apostle, who provided great leadership in what to do and how to do it. It is through the thirteen letters of Paul that we gather the most information as to how the New Covenant was spread to the known world. Luke, a close associate of Paul, became one of the major writers of the New Testament giving us the Gospel of Luke and the Book of Acts.

ACTS

The Gospel of Luke was written to tell the story of Jesus and the Book of Acts to detail the lives of the apostles in service to the gospel. Originally the two books were presented as one but in the final presentation of the New Testament the two books were separated.

WHO?

Most scholars assume that Luke the Gospel writer was the author of the Book of Luke. In the original manuscript the books of Luke and Acts were together. It is assumed that whenever the author uses "we" in the story of Paul's travels he himself was traveling with Paul. In other places in the scriptures it is obvious that Luke was writing a second-hand report most likely from the words of Paul. In several of his letters, Paul tells us Luke was there.

WHAT?

Although the book was given the title "The Acts of the Apostles" it mostly tells the story of just two apostles, Peter and Paul. The book provides us with an account of much of Paul's life, which helps us better understand the thirteen letters that are included in the New Testament.

WHEN?

The Book of Acts concludes with Paul being under house arrest in Rome for two years. This would indicate that the book must have been written either in 60-61 A.D. If you believe there was yet a fifth journey back to Rome as some scholars do, then it could have been written in 64-65 A.D. If it had been written later you would assume the writer would have included the outcome of Paul's trial in Rome.

WHY?

The theme of the Book of Acts is best summarized in Acts 1:8:

"You will be my witnesses in Jerusalem and in all Judea and Samaria, and to the ends of the earth."

The Book of Acts specifically tells the story of the presentation of the gospel throughout Palestine, northward to Antioch, and from there westward, through Asia Minor and Greece, to Rome—the region that constituted the backbone of the Roman Empire.

WHERE?

The Book of Acts was most likely written in Rome, Caesarea by the Sea, or perhaps started earlier in one of those locations and finished in Ephesus after Paul's death. The fact that it doesn't include Paul's trial and the outcome is one of the mysteries of the book.

KEY SCRIPTURES IN THE BOOK OF ACTS

He said to them, "It is not for you to know times or periods that the Father has set by His own authority. But you will receive power when the Holy Spirit has come upon you, and you will be my witnesses in Jerusalem, in all Judea and Samaria, and to the ends of the earth." (Acts 1: 7-8)

So those who accepted His message were baptized, and that day about 3000 people were added to them. And they devoted themselves to the Apostles' teaching, to fellowship, to the breaking of bread, and to prayer. (Acts 2: 41-42)

Salvation is found in no one else, for there is no other name under heaven given to men by which we must be saved. (Acts 4:12)

"What must I do to be saved"? They replied, "Believe in the Lord Jesus, and you will be saved—you and your household." (Acts 16: 30-31)

ROMANS

The Book of Romans is unique in that it contains the entire scope of the gospel of Jesus. Paul wrote most letters to churches he had started and to church leaders he had trained. He had not visited Rome at the time this letter was written so he was motivated to write his message as fully and completely as possible. If one wanted to recommend just one book from the New Testament as a witness to the gospel of Jesus Christ, Romans would be an excellent choice.

WHO?

The Book of Romans was written by Paul the Apostle. He opens this letter to the churches in Rome with the words,

"Paul, a servant of Jesus Christ, called to be an Apostle, set apart for the gospel of God . . ."(Romans 1: 1.)

This was the way he started all of his letters, each one telling the reader who he was and the purpose of the letter. That was the custom of the day.

WHAT?

Paul most likely wrote to the church in Rome because he received a contact from there asking him to come to Rome to preach to them. Romans is written as it is because nine of his thirteen letters in the New Testament were written to places Paul had visited before, had preached to, and most likely he had originally organized their churches. He knew them and knew what he had previously taught them. That was not so with the church in Rome. He did not start that church and obviously felt the need to give them a very complete look at the full gospel of Jesus Christ.

WHEN?

Paul wrote Romans toward the end of his third missionary journey, probably in 57 A.D. At that time Paul had been on the road for more than a year and was anxious to get back to Jerusalem. He promised the Romans that he would make his next journey to Rome.

WHY?

Paul wrote the Book of Romans in order to give a complete testimony to the church in Rome about the gospel of Jesus Christ. Rome was the center of the political and economic world at that time in history. To have a growing, functioning church in the heart of the empire was a very positive development and Paul wanted them to know all he could teach. He intended to visit them in person and continue his teaching on site in the near future.

WHERE?

Paul had paused in his third missionary journey in Corinth, probably because the winter had come when the Aegean and Mediterranean seas were impassible for about six months each year. The little, round-bottom boats that were available for travel from port to port during that time in history could not handle the weather on the high seas. It is likely that the Book of Romans was at least partially written while Paul was living in Corinth. There were many languages and nationalities apparent in the census of that city. Corinth was a thriving city with an international population of more than 400,000 people and many more in the surrounding area. It was a city which Paul described as full of sin and immorality and much in need of the gospel. So, he stayed there for many months working with his hosts, Aquila and Priscilla. These two fellow workers were originally from Rome and could tell Paul of their friends and fellow Christians there.

KEY SCRIPTURES FROM ROMANS

I am not ashamed of the gospel, because it is the power of God for the salvation of everyone who believes: first for the Jew, then for the Gentile. (Romans 1:16)

Since all have sinned and fall short of the glory of God, they are justified by his grace as a gift, through the redemption which is in Christ Jesus. (Romans 3:23)

For the wages of sin is death, but the gift of God is eternal life in Christ Jesus our Lord. (Romans 6:23)

We know that in everything God works for good with those who love him, who are called according to his purpose. (Romans 8: 28.)

For I am convinced that neither death nor life, neither angels nor demons, neither the present nor the future, nor any powers, neither height nor depth, nor anything else in all creation, will be able to separate us from the love of God that is in Christ Jesus our Lord. (Romans 8:38-39)

If you confess with your mouth, "Jesus is Lord," and believe in your heart that God raised Him from the dead, you will be saved. (Romans 10:9)

1ˢᵗ CORINTHIANS

Problems in the church at Corinth were significant even though Paul spent more than eighteen months there creating churches and sharing the true gospel. The source of the problem was most likely the constant influx of people into that thriving crossroads of many nationalities, ethnic groups, and religions. At that time in history Corinth had more than 400,000 people and the population was constantly changing as a result of the fact that the city was a major crossroads for travel and trade within the Roman Empire.

WHO?

This letter was written by Paul the Apostle to the churches in Corinth. It was actually the second letter he wrote to Corinth. The first letter was mentioned in this book but was lost to us. The first verse of this letter tells us,

"Paul, called by the will of God to be an Apostle of Christ Jesus, and our brother Sosthenes." (1ˢᵗ Corinthians 1: 1)

The latter part of the verse is telling us that Sosthenes is with him in Ephesus as he writes this letter. We may assume that Sosthenes has traveled with Paul to Corinth before and is not a stranger to the church leadership in Corinth.

WHAT?

The purpose of the letter is to respond to some questions raised by the leadership of the churches in Corinth. During that time in history there was not one church in Corinth but several. Small groups met in homes or wherever they could find a common location. Their leadership was also factionalized and that led to the problem of false teachings. Issues raised in this letter include division among church members (1:10-24); immorality (5:6:12-20); legal issues with each other (6:1-8); false teachings about the Resurrection of the body (Chap. 15); and inappropriate practice of the Lord's Supper (11:17-34).

WHEN?

This letter to the Corinthians was written perhaps in 56 A.D. during his third missionary journey and before Paul came to Corinth early in 57 A.D. where he wrote his letter to the Romans.

WHY?

Paul is trying to help the church groups in Corinth stay in the center of the gospel. Remember that Corinth is right in the center of Greece, a country with a highly educated population that was very much into philosophical debate. They were very capable of recreating their own religious perspective, altering the basic teachings of Paul about Jesus, his death and Resurrection, and leading the church membership astray.

WHERE?

Paul is writing from Ephesus, a city that he visited on his second journey and a location that developed a very strong church, one that would prove very important in future years of Christian development. By this time in history, Ephesus is a city about ten miles inland but it can be reached either by land or by sea. Remember, Ephesus was a seaport city when Alexander the Great based his military fleet there 150 years before. Now, with the sediment pulled down from the mountains by the river that flowed through the city, it was an inland city but it still had easy access to the sea.

KEY SCRIPTURES FROM 1ST CORINTHIANS

I appeal to you, brethren, by the name of our Lord Jesus Christ, that all of you agree and that there be no dissensions among you, but that you be united in the same mind and the same judgment. (1st Corinthians 1:10)

When I came to you, brethren, I did not come proclaiming to you the testimony of God in lofty words or wisdom. For I decided to know nothing among you except Jesus Christ and Him crucified. (1st Corinthians 2: 1-2)

Jews demand miraculous signs and Greeks look for wisdom, but we preach Christ crucified: a stumbling block to Jews and foolishness to Gentiles. (1st Corinthians 1:22-23)

And if Christ has not been raised, our preaching is useless and so is your faith. (1st Corinthians 15: 14)

Now we see but a poor reflection as in a mirror; then we shall see face to face. Now I know in part; then I shall know fully, even as I am fully known. And now these three remain; faith, hope, and love. But the greatest of these is love. (1st Corinthians 12: 12-13)

For what I received I passed on to you as of first importance; that Christ died for our sins according to the Scriptures, that he was buried, that he was raised on the third day according to the Scriptures. (1st Corinthians 15:3-4)

2nd CORINTHIANS

Second Corinthians is Paul's effort to further clarify the issues faced by the church. It is likely that he sent Titus and, perhaps, Timothy to carry the letter and to help with the ministry there while he was traveling in another part of the empire.

WHO?

Paul wrote 2nd Corinthians during his third missionary journey. During that journey he spent several months at Ephesus where he had written 1st Corinthians. This letter followed a few months later.

WHAT?

When Paul wrote this letter to the churches of Corinth he had just talked to Titus who had come from Corinth with word that the previous letter had done lots of good. Unfortunately, Titus told him of problems still to be handled. In this letter Paul is attempting to justify his ministry to those who still doubted his sincerity. Also, there were still Jewish Christians, identified as Judaizers, who were intent on altering the qualifications for being a Christian to include the rituals and traditions of Judaism.

WHEN?

It is likely that Paul wrote 2nd Corinthians in the spring of 55 A.D. while he was visiting the churches of Philippi and Thessalonica.

WHY?

The letter we call 2nd Corinthians was actually the third letter written by Paul to the churches in Corinth. The first letter was mentioned in 1st Corinthians but was lost to us. Thus, this is the second letter of which we have a record, but it is actually the third letter. Evidently Paul's authority was still being questioned by some and many still questioned whether or not Paul was a genuine apostle of Christ. Thus, Paul felt compelled to write again. Much of this letter is a justification of Paul's missionary calling.

WHERE?

Paul wrote this letter while he was in Macedonia. He had spent approximately three years in Ephesus where he wrote 1st Corinthians. Toward the end of that time there was a great riot in Ephesus, the reasons for which we do not know. Unfortunately, Paul almost lost his life in the riot. Shortly afterward he decided to move on to Corinth and to visit the churches in Philippi and Thessalonica on the way. It was his plan to leave Macedonia and travel south to Corinth.

KEY SCRIPTURES FROM 2nd CORINTHIANS

He has made us competent as ministers of a New Covenant—not of the letter but of the Spirit; for the letter kills, but the Spirit gives life. (2nd Corinthians 3: 6)

For our light and momentary troubles are achieving for us an eternal glory that far outweighs them all. So we fix our eyes not on what is seen, but on what is unseen. For what is seen is temporary, but what is unseen is eternal. (2nd Corinthians 4: 17-18)

For Christ's love compels us, because we are convinced that one died for all, and therefore all died. And He died for all, that those who live should no longer live for themselves but for Him who died for them and was raised again. (2nd Corinthians 5: 14-15)

Therefore, if anyone is in Christ, he is a new creation; the old has gone, the new has come. (2nd Corinthians 5: 17)

GALATIANS

Most Biblical scholars believe Paul's letter to the churches of Galatia was the first he wrote to the many churches he established during his four missionary journeys. It was in Paul's letter to the Galatians that he first began the separation of the new gospel from the Jewish traditions and customs. Standard requirements of the Jewish religion such as circumcision and the traditional Jewish rituals were abandoned. Paul taught the necessity for a personal relationship with Jesus Christ.

WHO?

Paul wrote Galatians as his first recorded letter to the churches of Galatia, the region where he had made his first missionary journey. That journey to Galatia had been very successful and many churches were founded. This was a follow-up letter to the churches and the many new Christians there.

WHAT?

The letter contains much about the Judaizers and their attempts to alter the criteria for becoming a Christian. Paul pointed out that the rituals of Judaism had nothing to do with becoming a Christian while the Judaizers taught that new believers must first accept the traditional Jewish traditions and customs. Much was written about the freedom in Christ, the lack of ritual and rules, the dependence on a personal relationship with Christ.

WHEN?

Some say that this letter was written by Paul around 57 A.D., as he was traveling toward Corinth. Others believe that it was written much earlier, around 49 A.D., just after Paul's first missionary journey.

WHY?

It seemed that wherever Paul preached the Judaizers followed closely behind. Those who had accepted Paul's message of the gospel of Jesus Christ were evidently susceptible to the teachings of others as well. Paul was adamant that his calling was directly from God and this was the one and true gospel of Christ. The Judaizers were wrong in their teachings.

WHERE?

Some say that Paul was in Antioch of Syria at the north edge of the Holy Land when he wrote this letter but others say he was most likely in Ephesus or Macedonia. During most of his journeys he was plagued with the Judaizers who had followed him into Galatia and were hybridizing the gospel he had preached and taught to the churches there.

KEY SCRIPTURES FROM GALATIANS

Know that a man is not justified by observing the law, but by faith in Jesus Christ. (Galatians 2: 16)

I have been crucified with Christ and I no longer live, but Christ lives in me. The life I live in the body, I live by faith in the Son of God, who loved me and gave Himself for me. (Galatians 2: 20)

But the fruit of the Spirit is love, joy, peace, patience, kindness, goodness, faithfulness, gentleness and self-control. Against such things there is no Law. (Galatians 5: 22-23)

Carry each other's burdens, and in this way you will fulfill the law of Christ. (Galatians 6:2)

For as many of you as were baptized into Christ have put on Christ. There is neither Jew nor Greek, there is neither slave nor free, there is neither male nor female; for you are all one in Christ Jesus. (Galatians 8: 27-28)

EPHESIANS

Ephesus was a favorite location of Paul's. He had visited there several times, often staying several months. He had many friends and followers there. Toward the end of his ministry he left Timothy, who he had called his beloved son, there to minister to the church and its growing congregation.

WHO?

Paul wrote this letter from prison to the Ephesians whom he regarded as the most steadfast of the churches he had established throughout the Middle East. The writer of Ephesians is obvious by the greeting and the closing, both standards of Paul's writing.

WHAT?

Paul spent much of his ministry teaching Gentiles that they could be Christians without becoming Jewish converts. This is another letter written to clarify some of the differences between the Jewish and Christian beliefs.

Paul taught Gentile Christians to stand up for their liberties in Christ. He did not want to see two churches, one of Christian Jews and one of Christian Gentiles. When Paul took the gifts of money and goods from the Gentile Christians to the Jewish Christians in Jerusalem he hoped it would help to break down the wall between the two groups that always seemed to be present.

WHEN?

The letter to the Ephesians was probably written while Paul was in Rome under house arrest and, thus, the date of the writing would have been between 60-63 A.D. However, there are some scholars who believe the letter was written later, perhaps around 64-65 A.D., when Paul may have been back in Rome again under arrest by the Romans. In order for the later date to be accurate there would have to have been a fifth missionary journey, this one back to Rome. There is conjecture but no scripture to support the later date.

WHY?

Paul wanted all to know that the gospel of Jesus Christ was so inclusive that in Him there was room for people of all different races, viewpoints, and prejudices. In short, Christ is the one who has the power to solve all the problems of mankind and to bring all social and family life into unity and harmony with God.

WHERE?

There is a major disagreement between scholars on where Paul was when he wrote this letter. Some say that he would not have written a letter to the church at Ephesus if he was in Ephesus and so he must have been in Rome. The Book of Acts, on the other hand, tells us the story of Paul going to Rome for the first time and Luke's company later in Paul's ministry. This writer thinks Paul was, in fact, in jail in Rome, perhaps on the first of two trips to Rome as guests of the Roman military. The scriptures list only one trip to Rome but there is evidence that, perhaps, Paul was there twice, first in 60 A.D. and then later, during the major persecution that followed the Emperor Nero's burning of Rome in 63 A.D.

KEY SCRIPTURES FROM EPHESIANS

Now to Him who is able to do immeasurable more than all we ask or imagine, according to His power that is a work within us, to Him be glory in the church and in Christ Jesus throughout all generations, for ever and ever! Amen. (Ephesians 3: 20-21)

In your anger do not sin: Do not let the sun go down while you are still angry, and do not give the devil a foothold. (Ephesians 4:26-27)

Finally, be strong in the Lord and in His mighty power. Put on the full armor of God so that you can take your stand against the devil's schemes. (Ephesians 6: 10-11)

PHILIPPIANS

The letter to the church at Philippi was written to the first church Paul established in Europe. He visited there during his second missionary journey in the company of Luke, Silas, and several others. His letter indicates that he had a warm feeling toward the people of Philippi and he returned to see them on his third journey.

WHO?

Paul's greeting at the beginning of this book makes it clear who is writing it.

"Paul and Timothy, servants of Christ Jesus, to all the saints in Christ Jesus who are at Philippi, with the bishops and deacons: Grace to you and peace from God our Father and the Lord Jesus Christ." (Philippians 1: 1-2)

WHAT

Paul had established the churches of Philippi around 51 A.D when he was on his second missionary journey. It was the first church he had established in Europe (Macedonia). Luke may have lived there or close by during that time in history practicing medicine in that locale. The Book of Acts tells us that he was with Paul while he was in Troas, Philippi and Thessalonica.

The Philippians had offered Paul money to help with his missionary journeys and Paul had accepted. Paul did not normally accept payment for his preaching and missionary work because he didn't want his motives to be misinterpreted. However, he did accept money at least twice from the churches in Philippi, perhaps the purest of all the churches he had established. This letter talks of many subjects, including his appreciation to them for providing financial support for his work.

WHEN?

The letter to the churches of Philippi was written around 62 A.D. Paul tells the churches in Philippi that he is in prison.

WHY?

In Paul's letter to the churches of Philippi he tells them that he appreciated receiving the money, not so much because he needed it, though he did need it badly (Philippians 2: 25), but because it gave them a share in the rewards for his work that would be credited to their account. Because they supported him, his work was theirs. In the final day they would be rewarded for the multitudes of souls they had helped him to save. This is one of the major justifications for unified giving among church groups for missions.

WHERE?

Paul could have been in Ephesus, Rome, or Caesarea by the Sea when he wrote this letter. There are no real clues in the writing and Bible scholars disagree.

KEY SCRIPTURES FROM PHILIPPIANS

But one thing I do: forgetting what is behind and straining toward what is ahead, I press on toward the goal to win the prize for which God has called me heavenward in Christ Jesus. (Philippians 3: 13-14)

Do not be anxious about anything, but in everything, by prayer and petition, with thanksgiving, present your requests to God. And the peace of God, which transcends all understanding, will guard your hearts and your minds in Christ Jesus. (Philippians 4: 6-7)

I can do everything through Him who gives me strength. (Philippians 4: 13)

COLOSSIANS

When Paul wrote his letter to the Colossians he was writing to a church he had never visited. It was obvious he was introducing himself at the same time he was presenting the gospel to that congregation.

WHO?

It is clear by the greeting at the beginning that this letter to the church at Colossae was written by Paul, probably while he was in prison in either Rome or Caesarea by the Sea.

WHAT?

The letter to the churches of Colossae was one of the letters that was written to several churches to combat what later came to be known as "The Colossian Heresy." The church at Colossae was not started by Paul but, instead, by one of his followers called Epaphras. Paul evidently wrote four letters during his stay in prison, three besides the one to the churches of Colossae. The letters to the churches of Philippi and Ephesus were very different from this one to the Colossians, who were battling some serious doctrinal problems.

WHEN?

It is likely that Colossians was written in the period of 59-61 A.D.

WHY?

The Colossian Heresy was a combination of several different religions inter-mingled into one philosophy. It was a mixture of Greek, Jewish, and Oriental religions, a sort of higher-thought cult that presented itself as the true doctrine of the Messiah. It called for the worship of angels as intermediaries between God and man. It insisted on the strict observance of certain Jewish requirements, almost to the point of the approach taught by the Jewish converts to Christianity who believed that you must first be a Jew before you could be a Christian.

WHERE?

Many of the Biblical scholars think Paul was in Rome under house arrest when he wrote this letter. Others think he was in Caesarea by the Sea. No one knows for sure. However, this writer believes that the preponderance of evidence indicates that he may have been in jail in Caesarea or, perhaps, in Ephesus at a time when the scriptures did not make note of it. Remember, the scriptures tell us of a time of major tumult in Ephesus that threatened Paul's life. He might have been jailed for a time there though there is no scripture to support this theory. Three other letters were written about the same time, one each to the churches at Philippi and Ephesus and the letter to Philemon about the slave Onesimus.

KEY SCRIPTURES FROM COLOSSIANS

And so, from the day we heard of it, we have not ceased to pray for you, asking that you may be filled with the knowledge of His will in all spiritual wisdom and understanding, to lead a life worthy of the Lord, fully pleasing to Him, bearing fruit in every good work and increasing in the knowledge of God. (Colossians 1: 9-10)

Christ in you, the hope of glory. (Colossians 1: 27)

As therefore you received Christ Jesus the Lord, so live in Him, rooted and built up in Him and established in the faith, just as you were taught, abounding in thanksgiving. (Colossians 2: 6-7)

Let the peace of Christ rule in your hearts, since as members of one body you were called to peace. And be thankful. (Colossians 3: 15)

Masters, treat your slaves justly and fairly, knowing that you also have a Master in heaven. (Colossians 4: 1)

1st THESSALONIANS

Paul first visited Thessalonica on his second missionary journey and he returned there on his third. Neither of his visits lasted very long, a matter of weeks. This letter emphasizes that Jesus is the Son of God who lived among men on earth for a time and the He is coming again.

WHO?

Paul founded the church in Thessalonica on his first trip through Macedonia. Shortly after he left there, he wrote back to the people. Again, one can read the greeting and know that Paul is the writer.

WHAT?

Paul was only in Thessalonica a short time and he had many believers there. He was accused by his Jewish detractors of "turning their world upside down." They drove him out of Thessalonica and he went on to Berea. He was also driven out of Berea and went on south to Athens. The word from Thessalonica was that many of the new believers were under persecution and some had been killed. Paul wrote this letter to tell them to stand firm in the word of Jesus.

WHEN?

It is likely that this letter was written in about 51 A.D.

WHY?

Paul's primary fear for the new Christians in Thessalonica was that they would give in to the persecution and walk away from the new Christianity. Through this letter Paul provided instruction regarding Godly living and urged them not to neglect their daily work. He tells the church that they can become a "model" church even though they are enduring persecution.

WHERE?

Paul was in Corinth when he wrote this letter and it had only been a few months since he had made his first visit to Thessalonica.

KEY SCRIPTURES FROM 1ST THESSALONIANS

May the Lord make your love increase and overflow for each other and for everyone else, just as ours does for you. May He strengthen your hearts so that you will be blameless and holy in the presence of our God and Father when our Lord Jesus comes with all His holy ones. (1ST Thessalonians 3: 12-013)

Be joyful always; pray continually, give thanks in all circumstances, for this is God's will for you in Christ Jesus. Do not put out the Spirit's fire; do not treat prophecies with contempt. Test everything. Hold on to the good. Avoid every kind of evil. (1st Thessalonians 5: 16-22)

For the Lord himself will descend from heaven with a cry of command, with the archangel's call, and with the sound of the trumpet of God. And the dead in Christ will rise first; then we who are alive, who are left, shall be caught up together with them in the clouds to meet the Lord in the air; and so we shall always be with the Lord. Therefore comfort one another with these words. (1st Thessalonians 4:16-18)

But as to the times and the seasons, brethren, you have no need to have anything written to you. For you yourselves know well that the day of the Lord will come like a thief in the night. (1st Thessalonians 5: 1-3)

For God has not destined us for wrath, but to obtain salvation through our Lord Jesus Christ, who died for us so that whether we wake or sleep we might live with Him. (1st Thessalonians 5: 9)

2nd THESSALONIANS

Paul's second letter to the Thessalonians restates much of what he said in the first with the additional admonition to "work and wait until He comes." In this letter he restates the words of John the gospel writer,

"...and if I go and prepare a place for you, I will come again..." (John 14: 3)

WHO?

This letter was written by Paul shortly after he had written the first letter to the Thessalonians. He had been gone from there for only a short time, maybe two months.

WHAT?

The message to the churches in Thessalonica is an echo of the first letter with "stand firm in the word" being the foundation, but also, "God will deal with your persecutors." As evidence of his concern Paul had sent Timothy back to Thessalonica to be of help and to assure the new Christians that Paul and the other missionaries had not abandoned them.

WHEN?

This letter was written about 51 A.D. from Corinth after Paul had previously visited Thessalonica, Berea, and Athens.

WHY?

Paul was trying to strengthen the resolve of the new Christians he had left to face the persecution in Thessalonica. He was concerned for them and wanted them to know he was still with them in spirit and, also, that God was their protector and He would see to their every need.

WHERE?

Paul was in Corinth when he wrote this letter. This was the end of his second missionary journey and he intended to leave for the Holy Land shortly. In fact, he remained in Corinth for many months waiting for the spring and better travel weather.

KEY SCRIPTURES FROM 2nd THESSALONIANS

We ought always to thank God for you, brothers, and rightly so, because your faith is growing more and more, and the love every one of you has for each other is increasing. (2nd Thessalonians 1:3)

Don't let anyone deceive you in any way, for that day will not come until the rebellion occurs and the man of lawlessness is revealed, the man doomed to destruction. He will oppose and will exalt himself over everything that is called God or is worshiped, so that he sets himself up in God's temple, proclaiming himself to be God. (2nd Thessalonians 2: 3-4)

But the Lord is faithful; he will strengthen you and guard you from evil. And we have confidence in the Lord about you, that you are doing and will do the things which we command. May the Lord direct your hearts to the love of God and to the steadfastness of Christ. (2nd Thessalonians 3: 3-5)

1st TIMOTHY

Paul's letter to Timothy is very much the letter of a father to a beloved son. His purpose is to help the young minister with the day-to-day problems of his church and congregation. We should note that this letter, like 2nd Timothy and Titus, are written to young pastors and not to the churches. Included are words of guidance for young men as well as young pastors.

WHO?

Paul is writing this letter to Timothy, whom he loved as a son. He was Paul's convert and he joined Paul on his second missionary journey. Paul had many companions on his journeys including Luke, Barnabus, Silas, and Titus but none like Timothy. He addressed him many times as his son in Christ.

WHAT?

Paul wrote this letter to establish some guidelines for the many small churches in Ephesus as well as to create some "authority" for Timothy and to establish him as his spokesman to the churches. Timothy was a native of Lystra in the middle of present-day Turkey. Paul met him there during his first missionary journey ten years before when he stayed in the home of Timothy's grandmother, Lois, and mother, Eunice's home. Timothy joined him on his second missionary journey.

WHEN?

It is likely that 1st Timothy was written during Paul's stay in jail in Rome, Caesarea by the Sea or, perhaps, from Macedonia during his third missionary journey. No one is exactly sure. The dates were most likely between 62 and 65 A.D.

WHY?

The purpose of this letter is to provide some instruction for Timothy in the handling of concerns and problems of the churches in Ephesus. There were many (maybe more than a hundred) pastors/elders/bishops in Ephesus during this period. This was the time of the major persecution shortly after Nero burned Rome and blamed it on the Christians. Many Christians were gathered into Ephesus under the protection of the church there. Paul was concerned that they have some on-site leadership and that is the role he created for Timothy. Thus, this letter was written to help Timothy with that major responsibility.

WHERE?

The date of this letter is not in dispute but the location of its writing is. Some scholars say Paul was imprisoned in Rome in 60-61 A.D. and this is when he wrote the letter. Others say he was imprisoned in Caesarea by the Sea during that period. However, this letter may have been written while Paul was in Macedonia shortly after having been released from prison in Rome, if you believe Paul was imprisoned in Rome twice as opposed to once, as some scholars do.

KEY SCRIPTURES FROM 1st TIMOTHY

The saying is sure: If any one aspires to the office of bishop, he desires a noble task. Now a bishop must be above reproach, the husband of one wife, temperate, sensible, dignified, hospitable, an apt teacher, no drunkard, not violent but gentle, not quarrelsome, and no lover of money. He must manage his own household well, keeping his children submissive and respectful in every way; for if a man does not know how to manage his own household, how can he care for God's church? If any one does not provide for his relatives, and especially for his own family, he has disowned the faith and is worse than an unbeliever. (1st Timothy 3: 1-5)

For everything God created is good, and nothing is to be rejected if it is received with thanksgiving, because it is consecrated by the word of God and prayer. (1ST Timothy 4: 4-5)

But godliness with contentment is great gain. For we brought nothing into the world, and we can take nothing out of it. But if we have food and clothing, we will be content with that. (1st Timothy 6: 6-7)

Let all who are under the yoke of slavery regard their masters as worthy of all honor, so that the name of God and the teaching may not be defamed. Those who have believing masters must not be disrespectful on the ground that they are brethren; rather they must serve all the better since those who benefit by their service are believers and beloved. (1ˢᵗ Timothy 6: 1-2)

2ⁿᵈ TIMOTHY

As Paul wrote this second letter to his "son in Christ" it is as if he knows his end is near. He is obviously pleased with his life in service to Christ and is content to pass on the heavy responsibility he carried to those willing to pick up the mantle of leadership. His letter is a good model for any father or grandfather to use when nearing the end of life and wanting to issue a challenge to the next generation.

WHO?

This letter was written by Paul just before his death. In 2ⁿᵈ Timothy 1: 1-2 the writer says, *"Paul, an Apostle of Christ Jesus by God's will, for the promise of life in Christ Jesus: To Timothy, my dearly loved child. Grace, mercy, and peace from God the Father and Christ Jesus our Lord."*

Thus, we know who wrote 2ⁿᵈ Timothy and as he tells us, it was written "by his own hand."

WHAT?

This letter is a mixture of strength and courage as well as a lament regarding frustration, fear, and hopelessness. Paul felt his own impending death and knew he was, perhaps, writing his last letter and making his last contact with his beloved Timothy.

In about 63 A.D. a great fire destroyed much of the city of Rome. This is the famous "Nero fiddled while Rome burned" event that shaped the persecution of the Christians for the next thirty years. Historians agree that Nero himself set the fires as the first major urban renewal project in the history of the world, an effort to beautify the city of

Rome. When the people reacted badly to his efforts, he blamed the Christians and thus set decades of persecution in motion.

WHEN?

Some biblical scholars believe that Paul was imprisoned in Rome in the early 60s A.D. and was released, then captured and imprisoned again in 65-67 A.D. as a part of the persecution following the burning of Rome which Nero blamed on the Christians. Others say that he might have been imprisoned first in Ephesus then later in Rome. No one knows for sure.

WHY?

Paul wrote this letter to Timothy, who was back in Ephesus, partially to make contact with his "son in Christ" and partially to let his many friends know of his situation in Rome. In 2nd Timothy, Paul gives us some of the best scripture for handling difficult situations and having faith in God no matter what happens.

WHERE?

There is little doubt that Paul was in Rome when he wrote this letter to Timothy back in Ephesus. During this period Paul was under house arrest and was waiting for his opportunity to appear in court and to appeal to the emperor for his release. That was not to be and most agree that Paul met his fate there in Rome shortly after this letter was written.

KEY SCRIPTURES FROM 2ND TIMOTHY

Remember Jesus Christ, risen from the dead, descended from David, as preached in my Gospel, the Gospel for which I am suffering and wearing fetters like a criminal. But the word of God is not fettered. Therefore I endure everything for the sake of the elect, that they also may obtain the salvation which in Christ Jesus goes with eternal glory. (2nd Timothy 2: 8-10)

But understand this, that in the last days there will come times of stress. For men will be lovers of self, lovers of money, proud, arrogant, abusive, disobedient to their parents, ungrateful, unholy, inhuman, implacable, slanderers, profligates, fierce, haters of good, treacherous, reckless, swollen with conceit, lovers of pleasure rather than lovers of God, holding the form of religion but denying the powers of it. Avoid such people. (2nd Timothy 3: 1-5)

All Scripture is God-breathed and is useful for teaching, rebuking, correcting and training in righteousness, so that the man of God may be thoroughly equipped for every good work. (2nd Timothy 3: 16 -17)

For I am already on the point of being sacrificed; the time of my departure has come.

I have fought the good fight, I have finished the race, I have kept the faith. Now there is in store for me the crown of righteousness, which the Lord, the righteous Judge, will award to me on that day—and not only to me, but also to all who have longed for His appearing. (2nd Timothy 4: 6-8)

TITUS

In this letter to Titus, Paul emphasizes the importance of good works. He does not tell Titus that one is saved by good works. Instead, he says we are saved *for* good works. Previously, Paul had sent Titus to become the pastor of the church in Crete. Later, he was bishop over all the churches established there.

WHO?

Paul wrote this letter to Titus when Titus was in Crete ministering to the churches there. Tradition tells us that after Paul's death Titus became bishop of the churches in Crete, lived to an advanced age and, unlike most of the other Christian leaders, died of natural causes.

WHAT?

Titus was a Greek Gentile who was converted, most likely, on Paul's second missionary journey. Paul used Titus in much the same way he used Timothy, as an aide on his journeys and as a messenger to the churches. The scriptures tell us that Titus was with Paul through much of his second and third missionary journeys. Titus was sent several places to carry Paul's messages, including Corinth and Crete. It is obvious that Paul thought Titus to be a very capable, wise, and tactful Christian leader.

This letter to Titus was sent for the purpose of supporting Titus as he ministered to the churches in Crete. The focus of the letter is the admonition to keep one's eye on the promise of eternal life, of doing good works here on earth, and on avoiding false teachers/prophets.

WHEN?

This letter was written by Paul in either 62 A.D. or 65 A.D. It is not known where Paul was when he wrote this letter though most believe he was either enroute to Rome or already there under house arrest.

WHY?

It is obvious that Paul loved Titus and had great respect for him. Crete was one of the first places where Paul had journeyed during his first missionary trip and he was pleased to send Titus back to Crete fifteen years after he had first visited that country to strengthen the ministry there. The letter to Titus focused on Paul's positive attitude toward the Christians there and his shared concern about the outcome of his going to Rome as a prisoner and his realistic assessment of his future.

WHERE?

We don't know where Paul was when he wrote the letter to Titus but evidence points to a time following his imprisonment at Caesarea by the Sea. If Paul was acquitted during his trial in Rome it is reasonable to assume that he traveled east after he was released and, perhaps, visited Crete at that time, leaving Titus behind there to minister to the churches. (If true, this would require that there was a fifth missionary journey back to Rome during the persecution of Christians following the burning of Rome in 63 A.D.) Later Paul sent for Titus to join him in Necropolis in Greece. The location of Paul during this time in his travels remains a mystery.

KEY SCRIPTURES IN TITUS

To the pure all things are pure, but to the corrupt and unbelieving nothing is pure; their very minds and consciences are corrupted. They profess to know God, but they deny Him by their deeds; they are detestable, disobedient, unfit for any good deed. (Titus 1: 15-16)

For the grace of God that brings salvation has appeared to all men. It teaches us to say "NO" to ungodliness and worldly passions, and to live self-controlled, upright and godly lives in this present age, while we wait for the blessed hope—the glorious appearing of our great God and Savior, Jesus Christ, who gave Himself for us to redeem us from all wickedness and to purify for Himself a people that are His very own, eager to do what is good. (Titus 2: 11-14)

Remind them to be submissive to rulers and authorities, to be obedient, to be ready for any honest work, to speak evil of no one, to avoid quarreling, to be gentle, and to show perfect courtesy toward all men. (Titus 3: 1-2)

I desire you to insist on these things, so that those who have believed in God may be careful to apply themselves to good deeds; these are excellent and profitable to men. (Titus 3: 9-10

PHILEMON

It is not widely understood why this letter is included among the books of the New Testament. It contains no theological truths. It is simply a letter from Paul to Philemon asking him to receive the run-a-way slave, Onesimus, as a brother in Christ and to send him back to Paul to help with the missionary work. Perhaps the book is intended as an example of love, forgiveness, and understanding.

WHO?

Paul tells us in the first few sentences of the letter that he wrote it. It is a unique letter written from jail to the benefit of a slave he had met while incarcerated.

WHAT?

The Book of Philemon is a simple letter to a brother in Christ about a slave who had run away. The admonition from Paul was for Philemon to forgive Onesimus, his slave, and to treat him as a fellow Christian. Yet, as it relates to the history of the Bible and the history of Christianity. This letter gives us a connection to Onesimus and, possibly, to the future development of the Christian church both in Ephesus and later as it spread through Europe.

While Paul was in jail he came to know Onesimus, who also was a prisoner. Onesimus became one of Paul's jailhouse converts and the run-a-way slave had told him about escaping from his master, Philemon, whose household was in Colossae. As chance (or God's direction) would have it, Paul knew of Philemon, probably from Titus who had visited the church at Colossae for Paul earlier. Paul did not know Philemon but through Titus he, obviously, knew of him.

WHEN?

Paul wrote this letter at the same time he wrote his letter to the church at Colossae, in about 60 A.D.

WHY?

Slaves were a part of accepted culture in the world of that time. About 60 percent of the Roman population was made up of slaves from various parts of the empire. Paul was trying to set a standard of behavior both for Christian free men and for slaves. How Christians treat others despite their station in life is of great significance to the understanding of Christ's intention for his followers. Further, Paul wanted Onesimus to become a free man and to come back and serve the cause either in Rome or in Ephesus.

Significant in the untold part of this story is a letter written about 73-75 A.D. from Ignatious, a pastor and Christian leader in Antioch during that time, to "The Great Bishop Onesimus" of Ephesus. It seems possible that the Onesimus of that letter may be the former slave who did, in fact, return to Ephesus as Paul had requested in his letter to Philemon. Years later he might have become the "Great Bishop" of the letter from Ignatious. As radio personality Paul Harvey used to say, that is "the rest of the story"!

WHERE?

Paul tells us that he was in jail when he wrote this letter. No one is sure just where. The letter is about the slave, Onesimus, who has run away from his master, Philemon. It somehow doesn't make sense that a slave could have gotten all the way to Rome or Caesarea by the Sea considering the borders to cross, and why would a slave run toward Rome? Some scholars believe Paul may have also been imprisoned in Ephesus, though there is no scripture to support this contention. That would have made more sense as per the location of Paul's meeting with Onesimus, since Colossae was only about eighty miles from Ephesus.

KEY SCRIPTURES IN PHILEMON

Grace to you and peace from God our Father and the Lord Jesus Christ . . . The grace of the Lord Jesus Christ be with your spirit. (Philemon 1: 3, 25)

Accordingly, though I am bold enough in Christ to command you to do what is required, yet for love's sake I prefer to appeal to you—I, Paul, an ambassador and now a prisoner also for Christ Jesus—I appeal to you for my child, Onesimus, whose father I have become in my imprisonment. (Philemon 1: 8-10)

Perhaps this is why he was parted from you for a while, that you might have him back for ever, no longer as a slave but more than a slave, as a beloved brother, especially to me but how much more to you, both in the flesh and in the Lord. (Philemon 1: 15-16)

Welcome him (Onesimus) as you would welcome me. (Philemon 1: 17)

HEBREWS

Some have referred to the Book of Hebrews as the Fifth Gospel. The first four describe Christ's ministry here on earth while this one describes his ministry in heaven at God's right hand. Other books of the Bible are about the apostles, the Roman oppressors, the responsibilities of Christians and their churches. This book is focused solely on Jesus and you will find Him on virtually every page.

WHO?

No one is sure who wrote the Book of Hebrews. In some ways the writing resembles that of the Apostle Paul. The original King James Version of the Bible called it "The Epistle of Paul the Apostle to the Hebrews." However, we may assume their attribution was only a guess. The evidence does not support Paul as the writer. The book does not have his traditional opening and closing. And, though Paul was a fine writer with very good skills in the Greek language, the Book of Hebrews is a step up in writing quality from Paul's thirteen letters. One historian strongly supports Priscilla as the author. She was a resident of the city of Corinth in Greece and was taught by Paul during his months-long stay there. If, in fact, Priscilla is the author, it would make sense that those collecting the books of the New Testament would not have put a woman's name on it. At that time in history, female authorship would have relegated the book to the trash heap, so the author's identity, if it was Priscilla, would have been kept secret.

WHAT?

The message of the book was to help the new Christians keep to the true faith, not to listen to false teachers, and to hold fast to the teaching of the disciples and close followers of Jesus. The book opens with the announcement of the superiority of the New Testament revelation by Jesus over Old Testament revelations by the prophets. In every way it proclaims the New Covenant as superior to the old.

WHEN?

Because of the content of the book, historians are able to date the writing to before the destruction of the Temple in Jerusalem by the Romans but after the time of the major persecution of Christians by Nero. That major persecution occurred after the burning of Rome in 63 A.D. So, the possible dates of writing were between 63 A.D. and 70 A.D.

WHY?

Those to whom the author of Hebrews is writing seem to have begun to doubt whether Jesus could really be the Messiah. This is because the Messiah of the Old Testament was to come as a militant king and destroy the enemies of the Hebrew Nation. Hebrews solves this problem by arguing that the Old Testament also foretold that the Messiah would be a priest and Jesus came first to fulfill this role. His role of being a king is yet to come, and those who follow Him should be patient and not be surprised that the time for Jesus as king is in the future and not now.

WHERE?

No one knows exactly where the Book of Hebrews was written. If Priscilla wrote the book, it may have been while she was in Ephesus under the protection of Bishop Onesimus in the 63-73 A.D. period. In truth, no one knows for sure.

KEY SCRIPTURES IN HEBREWS

For the word of God is living and active. Sharper than any double-edged sword, it penetrates even to dividing soul and spirit, joints and marrow; it judges the thoughts and attitudes of the heart. Nothing in all creation is hidden from God's sight. Everything is uncovered and laid bare before the eyes of Him to whom we much give account. (Hebrews 4: 12-13)

For we do not have a high priest who is unable to sympathize with our weaknesses, but we have one who has been tempted in every way, just as we are—yet was without sin. Let us then approach the throne of grace with confidence so that we may receive mercy and find grace to help us in our time of need. (Hebrews 4: 15-16)

After He was perfected, He became the source of eternal salvation to all who obey Him, and He was declared by God a high priest "in the order of Melchizedek." (Hebrews 5: 9)

For though by this time you ought to be teachers, you need someone to teach you again the basic principles of God's revelation. You need milk, not solid food. (Hebrews 5: 12)

Now faith is being sure of what we hope for and certain of what we do not see. (Hebrews 11: 1)

Now may the God of peace, who brought up from the dead our Lord Jesus—the great Shepherd of the sheep—with the blood of everlasting covenant, equip you with all that is good to do His will, working in us what is pleasing in His sight, through Jesus Christ, to whom be glory forever and ever. Amen. (Hebrews 13: 20-21)

JAMES

This book is the most practical of all the books in the New Testament regarding how a Christian is to serve God in his daily life. The emphasis throughout is serving God through serving our fellow man.

The key verse designed to motivate Christians follows.

"But, be ye doers of the word, and not hearers only." (James: 1:22)

WHO?

Scholars are not sure who wrote the Book of James. Two apostles were named James: one was the brother of John, the other was the son of Alphaeus (Matthew 10:2-3). One of Jesus' brothers was also named James. At first this brother did not believe that Jesus was the Messiah. He later believed and became prominent as the leading overseer of the Judean church (Acts 12: 17.) Some scholars regard James, the brother of Jesus, as the writer of the Book of James.

WHAT?

The Book of James was addressed to Christian Jews. It was written as a book of Christian proverbs that cover a number of subjects, all bearing on the practical aspects of the Christian life. In the text of his book, James talks about trials, perseverance, wisdom, and faith.

WHEN?

Christian tradition and the historian Josephus tells us that James was martyred in 62 A.D. Thus, his book had to be written prior to the beginning of the worst of the persecutions that began in 63 A.D.

WHY?

James wanted to let believers in Jesus know the importance of having a practical, living, everyday faith. For James, practical faith equaled good works, and those who professed faith yet had no good works could not presume that they were truly God's people. A part of the conflict between the words of James and those of the Gospel writers Matthew, Mark, Luke, and John had to do with the controversy of faith versus works for salvation.

WHERE?

No one knows for sure where James was when he wrote his book. However, since he was based mostly in Jerusalem while he was playing the role of bishop in charge of the Christian churches of Judea, it is likely that Jerusalem is the site of the writing of this book.

KEY SCRIPTURES IN THE BOOK OF JAMES

If any of you lacks wisdom, he should ask God, who gives generously to all without finding fault, and it will be given to him. But when he asks, he must believe and not doubt. (James 1: 5-6)

My dearly loved brothers, understand this: everyone must be quick to hear, slow to speak, and slow to anger, for man's anger does not accomplish God's righteousness. (James 1: 19-20)

What good is it, my brothers, if someone says he has faith, but does not have works? Can his faith save him? If a brother or sister is without clothes and lacks daily food, and one of you says to them, "Go in peace, keep warm, and eat well," but you don't give them what the body needs, what good is it? In the same way faith, if it doesn't have works, is dead by itself. (James 2: 14-17)

The prayer of a righteous man is powerful and effective. (James 5: 16)

1ˢᵗ PETER

This is the first of two letters written by Peter, the apostle. The theme of this book is using Jesus as a model for our lives,

"...to walk as Jesus did." (John2:6)

Peter emphasizes faith in God as the foundation of daily living and hope for the future as our constant motivation. To the devoted Christian he tells us that life gets sweeter every day and the very best is the reward at the end.

WHO?

There is little doubt that Peter the Apostle wrote 1ˢᵗ Peter and he tells us to whom he is writing. He begins his letter,

"Peter, an Apostle of Jesus Christ: to the temporary residents of the dispersion in the provinces of Pontus, Galatia, Cappadocia, Asia, and Bithynia, chosen according to the foreknowledge of God the Father and set apart by the Spirit for obedience and for the sprinkling with the blood of Jesus Christ. May grace and peace be multiplied to you." (1ˢᵗ Peter, 1:1-2)

WHAT?

Peter's first epistle contains many of the attributes of God, including his suffering and death for sinners, his resurrection and return in glory. It is an important text for understanding the Trinity. Peter dignifies all classes of human life by showing that living by the gospel makes a great difference in relationships. He includes a strong section teaching about salvation.

WHEN?

Scholars aren't sure when Peter wrote his first epistle, perhaps around 64 A.D. Peter's story is well known in the Bible, found in the Gospels of Matthew, Mark, Luke, and John as well as in Acts. It is likely that much of the Gospel of Mark was influenced by the teachings of Peter.

WHY?

First Peter was written to encourage Christians to be forward thinking, to live for the future. This book contains the most extensive New Testament development of a "theology of suffering," and it echoes the teaching from the Book of Job that God's glory is served even when suffering is permitted.

WHERE?

No one knows where Peter was when he wrote 1st Peter. If the date was approximately 64 A.D. as suggested previously, it is likely he was in Rome where his life was ended.

KEY SCRIPTURES IN THE BOOK OF 1st PETER

In this you greatly rejoice, though now for a little while you may have had to suffer grief in all kinds of trials. These have come so that your faith—of greater worth than gold, which perishes even though refined by fire—may be proved genuine and may result in praise, glory and honor when Jesus Christ is revealed. Though you have not seen Him, you love Him; and even though you do not see Him now; you believe in Him and are filled with an inexpressible and glorious joy, for you are receiving the goal of your faith, the salvation of your souls. (1st Peter 1: 6-9)

Therefore, get your minds ready for action, being self-disciplined and set your hope completely on the grace to be brought to you at the revelation of Jesus Christ. (1st Peter 1: 15)

So rid yourselves of all wickedness, all deceit, hypocrisy, envy, and all slander. Like newborn infants, desire the unadulterated spiritual milk, so that you may grow by it in your salvation. (1ˢᵗ Peter 2: 1-2)

Dear friends, I urge you as aliens and temporary residents to abstain from fleshly desires that war against you. Conduct yourselves honorably among the Gentiles, so that in a case where they speak against you as those who do evil, they may, by observing your good works, glorify God in a day of visitation. (1ˢᵗ Peter 2: 11)

2ⁿᵈ PETER

Peter's first letter was to encourage and motivate. This one is to warn against the dangers and snares that life brings and to keep one's eye on the eternal goal. The more one focuses on the model provided by the life Jesus lived the stronger one will grow in grace and knowledge.

WHO?

Second Peter opens with the statement,

"Simon Peter, a slave and an Apostle of Jesus Christ. To those who have obtained a faith of equal privilege with ours through the righteousness of our God and Savior Jesus Christ. (2ⁿᵈ Peter, 1: 1-2)

Thus, the scriptures are telling us who wrote 2ⁿᵈ Peter and who it was written for.

WHAT?

Peter tells us that God is the Father of Jesus, and He glorified His Son. God is the judge of all things human and super-human. Second Peter is the only book in the Bible that uses the full title, "our lord and Savior Jesus Christ," which is a magnificent confession by one who knew Him face-to-face during His earthly life. Peter described God's people as those *"who have obtained a faith of equal privilege,"* with the apostle. (2nd Peter 1:1).

WHEN?

Most scholars focus on the date, 67 A.D, as when this letter was written. Because of the content it is assumed that it was written after Paul's death in Rome.

WHY?

Peter was writing to warn Christians about false teachers who were presenting false doctrines to the churches. Peter wanted to re-explain a part of the gospel to arm the people with true knowledge as opposed to the heresy that was threatening the Christian movement. The false teaching he was most concerned about was related to Christ's return and the end times as taught by Peter and the other apostles.

WHERE?

No one is sure where Peter was when this letter was written. It is assumed that he probably was in Rome and already in prison. It is further assumed that Mark was with him and might have been playing the role of scribe for Peter in preparing this letter for the churches.

KEY SCRIPTURES IN 2nd PETER

For His divine power has given us everything required for life and godliness, through the knowledge of Him who called us by His own glory and goodness. (2nd Peter 1: 3)

For this very reason, make every effort to add to your faith, goodness; and to goodness, knowledge; and to knowledge, self-control; and to self-control, perseverance; and to perseverance, godliness; and to godliness, brotherly kindness; and to brotherly kindness, love. . .Therefore, my brothers, be all the more eager to make your calling and election sure. For if you do these things, you will never fall. (2ⁿᵈ Peter 1: 5-7, 10)

But there were also false prophets among the people, just as there will be false teachers among you. They will secretly bring in destructive heresies, even denying the Master who bought them, and will bring swift destruction on themselves. (2ⁿᵈ Peter 2: 1)

Dear friends , this is now the second letter I've written you: in both, I awaken your pure understanding with a reminder, so that you can remember the words previously spoken by the holy prophets, and the commandment of our Lord and Savior given through your Apostles. (2ⁿᵈ Peter 3: 1-2)

1ˢᵗ JOHN

This letter is not written to a particular church but, instead, to all. He is encouraging Christians to stay true to the new gospel and assures them they will have eternal life at the end of their challenge. By this time John was a very old man, perhaps well into his 80s. Over and over he uses the word "know," as in "Christians should be assured, should know that they have a unique relationship with God that will continue into eternity.

WHO?

John the Gospel writer and close friend of Jesus does not tell us he is the author of 1ˢᵗ John but the writing style and approach are so much like the fourth Gospel that the letter and the Gospel are generally acknowledged to be written by the same person. The letter was intended for Christians living in the Roman province of Asia, in and around Ephesus.

WHAT?

First John tells us that Jesus is the word of life who has come to earth and has been seen, heard, and touched. He reveals to us who God is and what God has done for our salvation. Jesus came to make it possible for us to have fellowship with the Father and to have fellowship with other believers.

WHEN?

John did not get back to Ephesus until after 80 A.D. so this letter was written after that time, but possibly before 90 A.D. While no one can be certain just when it was written, the decade of the 80s A.D. is a good estimate.

WHY?

John is writing mainly to combat the false doctrines of denying the incarnation of Jesus Christ coming to earth with real humanity and a truly physical body and denying that Jesus is the true Messiah, the long expected Christ. One of the great texts about salvation is found in 1st John 2:2.

WHERE?

It is likely that John the Gospel writer wrote this as a follow-up to his Gospel to the same people he addressed earlier. Ephesus was his home after he left his exile in Patmos so one can assume it was written in Ephesus while he was under the protection of the Christian church there.

KEY SCRIPTURES IN 1ST JOHN

But if we walk in the light as He Himself is in the light, we have fellowship with one another, and the blood of Jesus His Son cleanses us from all sin. (1st John 1: 7)

My little children, I am writing you these things so that you may not sin. But if anyone does sin, we have an advocate with the Father—Jesus Christ the righteous One. He Himself is the propitiation for our sins, and not only for ours, but also for those of the whole world. (1st John 2: 1)

This is how we are sure that we have come to know Him: by keeping His commandments. (1st John 2: 3)

You, dear children, are from God and have overcome them, because the one who is in you is greater than the one who is in the world. (1ST John 4: 5)

Dear friends, since God so loved us, we also ought to love one another. (1st John 4 :11)

2nd JOHN

John's second letter is unique in that it is the only letter in the Bible addressed to a woman. There are only thirteen versus in this book but the words "truth" and "love" are both used five times. John is saying that all teachings much be tested by scripture. When we walk in truth, in step with the scriptures, we will truly love one another.

WHO?

The letter claims to be written by "the Elder," but is otherwise unnamed. However, the style and content are so much like 1st John that these letters are acknowledged to be written by the same person. That person, of course, is John the Gospel writer and close associate of Jesus. It makes sense that John, writing after he came back from exile in Patmos, would have been in his 80s and, thus, could easily have referred to himself as "the Elder."

WHAT?

There is much in 2nd John related to discipleship, ethics, and morality. He stated that God is the Father of Jesus and is the one who has issued commands that His children are to live by. John's chief concern in the letter is to affirm that Christ has come in the flesh. Remember that John was a very old man by the standards of the time. To many of the Christians it seemed that he was going to live forever and be a follower of Christ who did not die.

WHEN?

John did not come back from Patmos until the 80s so the date of the writing is sometime between 80 A.D. and 90 A.D.

WHY?

2nd John was written to combat the same false doctrines that were written about in 1st John. The letters differ in that the first letter focused on the church congregation, the second on the family and personal setting.

WHERE?

This letter was most likely written in Ephesus after John came back from being exiled in Patmos. The letter is addressed to an unnamed Christian lady probably living somewhere in Roman Asia not far from Ephesus

KEY SCRIPTURES FROM 2ND John

I ask that we love one another. And this is love: that we walk in obedience to His commands. As you have heard from the beginning, His command is that you walk in love. (2 John 1: 5-6)

Many deceivers have gone out into the world; they do not confess the coming of Jesus Christ in the flesh. This is the deceiver and the antichrist. Watch yourselves so that you don't lose what we have worked for, but you may receive a full reward. (2 John 1: 7)

3rd John

In this letter to Gaius, a follower of Christ, John is telling him that he is a true example of Christ's teachings. Gaius was a man of means who had given his time, talent, and wealth to the Lord. John calls him a man whose nature is one of loving hospitality.

WHO?

The author of this letter is no doubt John the Apostle. He is writing to Gaius, a Christian living in Roman Asia somewhere not far from Ephesus.

WHAT?

John was writing mainly to advise Gaius about his responsibility to receive warmly a group of traveling ministers. He also was giving warning about the troublemaker, Diotrephes. In this letter John often used the expression "the truth." It is a paraphrase for "the gospel of Jesus Christ." His primary purpose was to smooth the way for the traveling ministers.

WHEN?

It is likely that the third letter was sent shortly after the first two sometime in the decade of the 80s. John was back from Patmos and was beginning to take some leadership within the church of Ephesus.

WHY?

John wrote to Gaius about the value of providing true hospitality to traveling Christian missionaries as they visited his locale. He commended such hospitality for the sake of the Gospel. He also warned about the troublemaker, Diotrephes, who had rejected the traveling ministers.

WHERE?

John was at home in Ephesus close by the church in that locale that had become a sanctuary for Christians during troubled times as the Romans persecuted Christians all across their empire.

KEY SCRIPTURES IN 3RD JOHN

I pray that you may enjoy good health and that all may go well with you, even as your soul is getting along well . . . .I have no greater joy than to hear that my children are walking in the truth. (3rd John 1: 2, 4)

Dear friend, you are showing your faith by whatever you do for the brothers, and this you are doing for strangers; they have testified to your love before the church. (3rd John 1: 5-6)

Dear friend, do not imitate what is evil but what is good. The one who does good is of God; the one who does evil has not seen God. (John 1: 11)

JUDE

The Book of Jude is a letter written in much the same model and spirit as 2nd Peter. He is warning of persons who have joined the church but are not true believers. He admonishes the church to beware of these false Christians who spread false doctrines.

WHO?

Jude identifies himself as "a slave of Jesus Christ and a brother of James." There were several named Jude in the New Testament, but the only one who was James' brother was also the brother of Jesus and the son of Mary and Joseph. He was writing to believers but we don't know their location.

WHAT?

Jude's letter focuses on the world view of revelation, authority, ethics, and morality. It especially emphasizes that God's revealed truth should not be altered. He condemns false teachers over and over and especially their motivation, which he identifies as greed and lust.

WHEN?

It is likely that this letter was written in the decade of 60-70 A.D. Again, we have no proof and nothing in the text gives us a clue as to when it was written.

WHY?

Jude wrote his letter to condemn false teachers who were teaching that as Christians they were free to sin since they had been forgiven and were under God's grace. Jude wanted his readers to oppose this teaching with the truth about God's grace.

WHERE?

We do not know where Jude was when he wrote this letter. It is possible he was in Jerusalem but we have no proof of his location.

KEY SCRIPTURES IN JUDE

Dear friends, although I was eager to write you about our common salvation, I found it necessary to write and exhort you to contend for the faith that was delivered to the saints once and for all. (Jude 1:3)

But you, dear friends, building yourselves up in your most holy faith and praying in the Holy Spirit, keep yourselves in the love of God, expecting the mercy of our Lord Jesus Christ for eternal life. (Jude 1: 17)

To Him who is able to keep you from falling and to present you before His glorious presence without fault and with great joy—to the only God our Savior be glory, majesty, power and authority, through Jesus Christ our Lord, before all ages, now and forever more! Amen. (Jude 1: 24-25)

REVELATION

Every book in the New Testament except this one tells either the story of the life of Christ or the efforts of his followers to spread the new gospel. Revelation, in contrast, is a book of prophecy. John was a very old man by the time he wrote Revelation. His goal was to tell Christians of the vision God had given to him about their future if they stayed faithful to the Christ of the scriptures.

WHO?

John the Gospel writer identifies himself as the writer of Revelation in the first verse of his book. He is writing to persecuted Christians living in seven cities in the Roman province of Asia. John tells us that God directed him to write this communication to these seven churches.

Left to his own devices John might have chosen others as an audience for his Revelation, but God chose these seven.

WHAT?

The Book of Revelation is a book of prophecy, a message to God's people exhorting them to remain faithful to Him. In many ways it has the properties of the writings of Isaiah and Jeremiah in that it predicts both near and remote future events. Though Revelation is written in Greek it is "weak" Greek, not as polished as most of the other books in the New Testament.

WHEN?

It is likely that Revelation was written between 80 A.D. and 90 A.D. and was the last book or letter we have evidence of that was written by John the Gospel writer and close associate of Jesus.

WHY?

John tells us that while he was on Patmos God appeared to him and gave him visions that he was instructed to write down. We may assume that all Bible books are inspired by God, but this one, more than any other, bears a sense of divine dictation. God wanted these messages delivered.

WHERE?

John tells us that these visions came to him while he was in exile and he was ordered to share them with the faithful Christians of the seven churches of Asia as designated. We do not know if they were delivered while John was still in exile or shortly after his return but we can be sure from John's own word that he wrote Revelation while on Patmos.

KEY SCRIPTURES FROM REVELATION

Blessed is the one who reads the words of this prophecy, and blessed are those who hear it and take to heart what is written in it because the time is near. (Revelation 1: 3)

"Look! He is coming with the clouds, and every eye will see Him, including those who pierced Him. And all the families of the earth will mourn over Him. This is certain. Amen." (Revelation 1: 7)

"I am the Alpha and the Omega," says the Lord God, "the One who is, who was, and who is coming, the Almighty." (Revelation 1:8)

Then I saw a new heaven and a new earth. . . And I heard a loud voice from the throne saying, "Now the dwelling of God is with men, and He will live with them. They will be His people, and God himself will be with them and be their God. He will wipe every tear from their eyes. There will be no more death or mourning or crying or pain, for the old order of things has passed away." (Revelation 21: 1, 3-4)

APPENDIX

The dictionary says that an appendix is material attached to the end of a manuscript that may supplement or add to the understanding of the text. The following is not a part of the foregoing but, instead, is a series of essays and additions on a variety of subjects that may be of interest to the reader. Much of the following deals with questions raised when one combines the study of history with the study of the scriptures.

In the conflict history of the church there were several "water-shed" events. One of those that had long term impact happened in German in the mid-1500s. Martin Luther opened the door to the Reformation when he tacked his 95 thesis onto the door of the church in Wittenburg, Germany. He was searching for discussion and debate on the subjects written into his thesis. It was not his intent to start a revolution within the Catholic Church or to create an entirely new approach to scripture. In truth, he did both.

The purpose for including the essays and other information in the Appendix of this book is similar to the intent of Martin Luther. Writing essays is an orderly way to search for understanding and to present items for discussion. The following contains much that constitutes such a search and there is no apology for statements and questions that can easily be identified as speculation. If no one ever took a position on an issue that is contrary to "conventional" thinking, the earth would still be flat and the sun would still revolve around the earth. Certainly, without such discussion it is not likely the truth or falsehood of an issue will ever be discovered.

You will notice some overlap of information in the essays since they were all written at different times for different audiences.

HOW SCRIPTURE IS AUTHENTICATED

When scholars study scripture they use a variety of devices to assure themselves that the passage they are researching is truly the word of God. Assumptions about the authenticity of an item in scripture are made if it appears to be logical and has support in authentic documents other than scripture, such as being noted in Roman history. For instance, we know that Jesus lived because his name and portions of his life are referred to not only in the New Testament but also in ancient Roman documents. We know that several wars/battles recorded in the Bible actually happened because they are also recorded in documents found in countries surrounding the Holy Land. Several individual scriptures and the entire Book of Isaiah can be found in the Dead Sea Scrolls, which date from the Bible era. Many of these archaeological treasurers are found on display today in a museum in Jerusalem.

The process for accepting books for inclusion in the Bible at the time it was created required that the book meet a list of criteria that made sense in that period just after Bible times. Those criteria are still accepted today. This process is called "canonization," a word that came from the root word "cane" or "reed" which was sometimes used as a measuring rod in Bible times. These criteria follow:

1. The book had to have wide acceptance among the churches. Regional acceptance was not adequate.

2. Books had to date to the Apostolic Era, that period just after the death and resurrection of Christ, and be connected to an apostle either by direct authorship or association, such as Mark with Peter and Luke with Paul.

3. The books had to prove beneficial for the churches that heard them read. The books that are in our canon are there because they could not be kept out—the people recognized their authority as being from God.

4. The books had to be suitable for public reading in the churches.

There are other books written that could have been in the Bible but aren't. The reason for excluding them is different with each possibility. Some were not included because they cannot be authenticated. Some of those documents were not available to the evaluators when they were together making the decisions about what to include. There have been multiple gatherings for the canonization of scripture where decisions were made on which books to include. The first of these was in 350 A.D. Other, later, gatherings were held by different Christian groups to formalize the Bible that would be used by their denomination. That is why the Catholic Bible has additional books that are not in the Bible used by most Protestant denominations. In recent years books reported to be written by the apostles Thomas and Judas have been discovered. Neither is in the Bible because 1) they have not been authenticated and, 2) they were not available when such decisions were being made. The King James Version of the Bible was put together about 1,600 years after the death and resurrection of Christ and it is the foundation Bible used by most Protestant groups.

A second criterion for inclusion in the Bible is that the book must come from the Apostolic Era, that period just after the death and resurrection of Christ, and be connected to an apostle so that authorship could be directly linked to Jesus or someone who had been a close follower of Jesus. Thus, the books of Matthew, Mark, and John were all written by apostles who had contact with Jesus. Luke also was there during that time, though he could not be directly linked to Jesus. His link was with Paul and the other apostles, as well as Mary, the mother of Jesus.

Matthew, Mark, Luke, and John all qualified. Paul appeared on the scene shortly after and was directly linked to Jesus in a unique way. Paul met Jesus on the road to Damascus and was linked with the apostles from that time forward. His writings became the foundation of our church organization and through him many of the standards for Christian behavior and responsibility were set.

The words "disciple" and "apostle" are often used interchangeably and most of the time that is correct, but not always. An apostle is a follower of Jesus who knew Him personally and was sent out to preach and heal by Jesus. A disciple is one who is a follower of Jesus who may not have known Jesus personally. Every Christian can be described as a disciple. All of the original "twelve" chosen by Jesus were apostles. Of the others who followed, only Paul claimed to be an apostle. He could have said, "I am an apostle if anyone is by virtue of my meeting with Jesus on the road to Damascus. I saw Him face to face and He directed me in a way that changed my life."

A book that is currently included in the Bible may be said to have been canonized. Once a book is accepted, every scripture within the book is accepted as well. At some point in the future there may be another conference for the canonization of scripture. Until that time, we have the scriptures as they stand.

IMPORTANT DATES IN THE HISTORY OF JERUSALEM

1. 2200 B.C.: Jerusalem (originally called Salem) was first listed in the Bible in Genesis 14:18. It is obvious that Salem already existed when Abraham arrived in the mountainous region north of Jerusalem as a result of his direction from God. That was approximately 2200 B.C.

2. 1420 B.C.: Jerusalem was a major walled city when Joshua brought the Hebrew Nation across the Jordan River and began his conquest in approximately 1420 B.C. Joshua did

3. not attack Jerusalem and left it standing as a Canaanite city surrounded by Israeli settlements and the remnants of his army.

4. 1030 B.C.: David conquered Jerusalem, but not by siege or by attacking its formidable walls. He knew he had little chance of taking the city unless he could get a force inside its gates. Jewish tradition tells us that he entered Jerusalem by taking a group of his best soldiers in through an underground tunnel that supplied Jerusalem with water and then climbing up through the well into the city. From there David's troops opened the gates and let his army in.

5. 980 B.C.: Solomon built the Temple in Jerusalem in approximately 980 B.C. Remember that David wanted to build God's Temple but God told David,

"You are not to build a house for My name because you have shed so much blood on the ground before Me." (1st Chronicles 22:8)

Thus, that task fell to his son Solomon.

6. 586 B.C.: The first destruction of the Temple in Jerusalem occurred with the conquest of the Babylonians in approximately 586 B.C. The Temple was rebuilt in approximately 435 B.C. The second destruction of the Temple was initiated by King Herod, who tore it down and rebuilt it in the decade before the birth of Christ. The third destruction of the Temple took place in 70 A.D. by the Romans who had come to put down a revolt which in Roman history was called, simply, the Jewish Revolt. Since 70 A.D. the Temple has not been reconstructed.

7. 1947 A.D: The wailing wall, one of the most famous Jewish shrines, is the original west wall of the Temple built by Solomon. It dates from the time when it was believed that the God of the Jews lived in the Temple. The wall was excavated in 1947 and left in its present state.

   Jerusalem was not part of the land given to Israel when a homeland was created for the Jews after World War II. The Jews took Jerusalem by force when they defeated the Arab Union after being attacked following the creation of Israel in 1947. To reach the wall of Solomon's Temple, the Israeli government excavated approximately 40 meters below ground level. That is why, in pictures taken today, all of the buildings and the grounds around the Wailing Wall appear to be above it.

GENESIS AND CONTROVERSY

This writer feels safe in saying that as much as half of the controversy related to the entire Bible can be found in the first eleven chapters of the Book of Genesis. In those eleven chapters there are many stories, declarations, and sources of information that raise questions that, short of talking with God Himself, we cannot answer. One of these sources of controversy is the story of the Great Flood.

Was the great flood universal, covering the entire earth, or did it cover just the portion of the world known to the ancestors of the Hebrew Nation? Did the animals saved by Noah's Ark come from the entire world or just the surrounding region? Could the water that was produced by the...

"...floodgates of heaven and the springs of the deep..." (Genesis 7: 11)

... cover the entire world including the 29,000-foot Mount Everest or did the waters cover just the hills of the Tigris and Euphrates Valley? (Note the difference between the King James Version of the Bible and later translations regarding the use of the word "mountains" as opposed to "hills.")

It is generally agreed by most Biblical scholars that Moses wrote the first five books of the Bible. These are Genesis, Exodus, Leviticus, Numbers, and Deuteronomy. Of these five books, Moses was an eye witness to the events recorded in the last four. The Book of Genesis was written by Moses from word-of-mouth stories told through generations of the elders of the Hebrew Nation. After more than 400 years in captivity in Egypt, the Children of Israel wandered in the wilderness for another 40 years, prior to entering the Holy Land.

Thus, Moses was writing the Book of Genesis with a major disadvantage. He not only had not witnessed any of the events he was writing about, he was hearing about them for the first time from people who had not witnessed them either. Moses was raised in Pharaoh's palace as a royal prince and, when the stories were told to him by his people in the wilderness, it was the first time he had heard them. Thus, the stories were not just second hand, they were much farther down the line, having been passed down through sixteen or eighteen generations. This was their oral history for generations and centuries.

Prior to their captivity in Egypt the ancestors of the Hebrew Nation were living in the Holy Land, prior to that in Haran, and prior to that in Ur. Thus, it was approximately eighteen generations from the time

Abraham moved from Ur up the Tigris and Euphrates River Valley. The time of Noah and the flood was at least three generations before the time God asked Abraham to move his family *"to a land He would show him" (Genesis 12:1).* Thus, more than 500 years had passed between the flood and the telling of the stories. There were no eye witnesses. Even the names of the rivers and landmarks may have changed or been forgotten.

If one can identify the Book of Genesis as one of inspired oral history, a key question is, "Is it the history of the world or the history of the Hebrew Nation?" If it was the history of the world, as some believe, there are many things to take on faith regarding the stories of Adam and Eve, their sons and wives, Noah and the Ark, etc. If the Book of Genesis is a word-of-mouth history of the Hebrew Nation, then many of the unanswered questions of the first eleven chapters of Genesis can be answered by identifying the others who enter the story from time to time (the wives of Adam and Eve's sons, etc.) as people of other nations.

For most of the existence of the more conservative denominations of Christianity, Genesis has been considered a word-of-mouth history of the world. Many other denominations view Genesis as a history of the Hebrew Nation. In recent years literature and other support materials published by some of the more conservative denominations have been evolving toward the perspective that Genesis is a history of the Hebrew Nation.

The position a person takes as an individual on this issue is key to how the first eleven chapters of Genesis are viewed. One of the former instructors of Old Testament at a well-known Christian university often dealt with such issues by saying, "Well, some would say this, but others would say that." He was a master of making sure that students never knew what he, personally, thought on a controversial issue. The desire of this writer is to make the reader think about the issues that are clearly stated but, also, to think about the less clearly stated issues of how things might have been.

We each arrive at our own answers, opinions, and speculations regarding the mystery of how a powerful God created the world.

WHERE WAS THE GARDEN OF EDEN?

One of the great mysteries of the past six thousand years is the location of the Garden of Eden that is described in the Book of Genesis. There has been much speculation over the years about its location and so-called experts have located it in such diverse locations as Mesopotamia in the Middle East and the Sudan of Africa. One of this writer's favorite stories comes from a time living on the island of Sri Lanka near the coast of India. There, local folklore among the Christian population assumed that since their island was obviously a paradise, Eden must have been located in Sri Lanka.

Here is what the scriptures say:

Now the Lord God had planted a garden in the east, in Eden; and there he put the man he had formed. And the Lord God made all kinds of trees grow out of the ground—trees that were pleasing to the eye and good for food. In the middle of the garden were the tree of life and the tree of knowledge of good and evil. A river watering the garden flowed from Eden; from there it was separated into four headwaters. The name of the first is the Pishon; it winds through the entire land of Havilah, where there is gold. The gold of that land is good; aromatic resin and onyx are also there. The name of the second river is the Gihon; it winds through the entire land of Cush. The name of the third river is the Tigris; it runs along the east side of Asshur. And the fourth river is the Euphrates. (Genesis 2: 8-14)

From what is said in the scriptures the site can be placed somewhere close to the Tigris and Euphrates rivers that run through Mesopotamia. There is one obvious problem with that location: the scripture says that a river flowed out of Eden. In fact, if the location is along the Tigris and Euphrates river valleys, the river is flowing through Eden. Should a location at the upper end of the Fertile Crescent be considered? That would be consistent with the location of the two rivers but there do not appear to be two other rivers that fit the story.

Three possible locations of the Garden of Eden will be examined. As is always true in such cases, the reader will have to make his/her own decision on which is the correct choice. Or, perhaps, none of the three will seem to meet the scriptural description.

1. The Garden of Eden was located at the headwaters of the Nile River in Africa.

So much of the Book of Genesis seems to have a relationship with what the Children of Israel knew in Egypt. In Egypt there is one dominant body of water, the Nile. It runs out of the Sudan and, indeed, four major rivers (and several smaller ones) come together to form the Nile. Those rivers do not have the familiarity of the Tigris and Euphrates rivers to us. However, it is not beyond our imagination to think that while living in Egypt the Children of Israel heard stories of how God created man and woman at some mysterious place where the "Mother of Waters" (the Nile) began.

In fact, the Tigris and Euphrates rivers, well known to those who lived in Ur, ancient Sumer and Babylon, were probably not known at all to Moses and his people except in stories passed down through the generations from parent to child, word-of-mouth. We might suspect that someone added the specific names of the rivers in a later edition of the Book of Genesis.

2. The Garden of Eden was located at the mouth of the Tigris and Euphrates rivers close to present-day Kuwait.

Many have suggested that the area south of the mouth of the Tigris and Euphrates rivers in an area now underwater in the Persian Gulf would fit the description if we could reverse the scriptures so that the rivers flowed into rather than out of the Garden of Eden. In that time several thousand years ago the water level in the oceans was not as high as now. The upper end of the Persian Gulf valley would have been an ideal climate for the tropical region described in the scriptures.

Unfortunately, the rivers run into and not out of the region and there are only two of them instead of the four specified in Genesis. Of course, two other rivers might have existed then but, still, they would have been running into Eden instead of out of that lovely garden.

3. The Garden of Eden was located in the Holy Land in what is today northern Israel and southern Lebanon.

In order for the Holy Land to have been the Eden of the Bible, several things would have to be very different from today. Today, the land is a high plateau and there is no source of water that would have created the headwaters of the four rivers. However, geologists tell us that major changes have occurred from that time several thousand years ago. Some of those happenings follow:

1. The Dead Sea Rift was created by a collision of the African and Arabian Tectonic Plates. When that collision took place it caused the Arabian plate to slide above the African plate thus lifting the entire northern region of the Arabian Peninsula. What had been an almost tropic area with adequate rainfall and a significant river became dry desert land.

2. Before the creation of the rift, the sandy soil along the coast of the Mediterranean may have felt pressures caused by the weight of the sea pushing water under the land mass to rise as springs inland at one or more locations. (Such still occurs at many locations along oceans and rivers throughout the world.) Thus, a major source of water may have been available in the area of the Holy Land, enough to have supplied a major river flowing north along the base of Mt. Hermon and south through the area currently occupied by the Dead Sea.

3. The scriptures specify the headwaters of four rivers. The Tigris and Euphrates both begin just on the east side of Mt. Hermon and might have been supplied by the spring water from the Holy Land. The third river, the Gihon, that the scriptures describe as winding through Cush, which is located on both sides of the Red Sea could well have been the southern run-off of the river that started in the center of the Holy Land. As previously stated the ocean water levels were significantly lower than today so such a river would have run through the Red Sea valley which would have split the land of Cush right down the middle.

4. That leaves only the location of the Pishon River to resolve. The scriptures tell us that river would wind through the land of

Havilah. Havilah was located in the upper half of the Arabian Peninsula and was the region that was raised by the collusion of the two Tectonic Plates. Today, there is no river and the land is an arid desert. However, satellite images of the region reveal that there is an ancient river bed that runs from the Red Sea Valley directly across the northern region of the Arabian Peninsula and would have emptied into the Persian Gulf near the mouths of the Tigris and Euphrates rivers. This may be the Pishon River that the scriptures describe.

So, is the northern region of the Holy Land the location of the legendary Garden of Eden? If it is, one could read further in the Book of Genesis to the story of Abraham and surmise that when God directed him to pick up his belongings and his family and "move to an area I will show you" he might have been moving Abraham and his wife Sari back to the Garden of Eden where he had originally placed Adam and Eve. One could say that God originally intended to populate his planet and grow his chosen people from the Garden of Eden. It just took more time to effect because sin reared its ugly head.

WHERE IS THE ARK OF THE COVENANT?

No object in the history of man has been more sought after, more debated, more coveted nor more valuable than the Ark of the Covenant. Its description in the Book of Genesis is very explicit and so we know exactly what it looked like, its purpose, and how carefully Moses took care of it. Unfortunately, there is no record of anyone having seen it for more than 2,500 years. How it disappeared and where it is today is still a matter for debate and conjecture. (That is true no matter what the Indiana Jones movies would have you believe!)

1. IT IS A BOX

The English word "ark" has many meanings. The Hebrew word is *aron,* which means "box." The word "ark" that refers to Noah's Ark is *tebah* and is a different word with a different meaning in Hebrew. The purpose of the Ark of the Covenant was to provide a place to store and protect the Ten Commandments, which were the foundation of the covenant between God and the Hebrew Nation.

2. THE ARK'S CONSTRUCTION

The ark was designed by God, but built by man, much as Noah's Ark was. The craftsmen who built it were very skilled at both woodworking and gold crafts. The plan for the ark was recorded in Exodus, the 25th chapter and was given directly to Moses. The ark was to be approximately 3.75-by-2.25-by-2.25 feet. Thus, it wasn't much larger than a travel trunk or a good-sized hope chest. (A very similar chest was found in the tomb of King Tut, one of the young pharaohs in Egypt. That chest is almost the same size but has the Egyptian's dog god on top of it.)

The construction plan called for the ark to be built out of acacia wood, a thorny tree with rough bark found in the Sinai Desert area. The wood surface was to be covered in gold both inside and out, and it was to have a gold molding around it. The gold was probably gold leaf, very thin. Since they had to carry it everywhere they went, making the box solid gold was probably not an option since it would have been too heavy to carry. The lid on top was to have two cherubim on it with their wings raised and extended over the lid.

3. THE SYMBOL OF GOD'S PRESENCE

To the Hebrew Nation, the Ark of the Covenant was the symbol of God's presence among the Children of Israel. As long as it was there and led them, they knew that God was with them. When Moses moved his camps, the ark was always carried in front of the people. When they camped they placed the ark in the center of the camp, posted soldiers around it, and set the camp up so invaders would have to get through the entire company before getting to the ark.

Often when they went to war, the ark was carried onto the battlefield with them. That led to their losing the ark to the Philistines later in their history. The Philistines offered it back to them when plagues and strange illnesses affected the Philistines wherever they tried to keep it. When David became king of the Hebrew Nation, he retrieved the ark and brought it to Jerusalem.

Unfortunately, he had no temple for it to reside in and it stayed at the edge of the city in the home of a Levite priest for a time and then it was kept in a tent.

Following David's reign, Solomon built his beautiful temple, a spectacular memorial to God, and moved the ark into the part of the temple that was called the Holy of Holies.

4.   HOW THE ARK WAS LOST

No one seems to know for sure how the ark was lost. However, there is a traditional story that when the Babylonians were coming to conquer the city of Jerusalem Jeremiah took the ark out to the wilderness on the east side of the Jordan and hid it in a cave. The scripture tells us that Jeremiah escaped to Egypt for a time but the scripture does not report any additional travels of either Jeremiah or the Ark of the Covenant. However, tradition in Israel says that Jeremiah came back to Jerusalem a few years later and may have retrieved the ark from its hiding place.

Some believe that Jeremiah came back from Egypt and led a group of his followers to Mecca (before the creation of the religion called Islam) and then to Yemen. After several years in each place they evidently embarked by boat to Ethiopia, where they moved inland and south. Today, there are approximately 70,000 Jews who live in the area at the north edge of South Africa and the southern edge of Zimbabwe. These are the so-called, Lost Tribe or "Black" Tribe of Israel. They still follow all of the Jewish customs 2,500 years later. Archeologists did not know whether to accept their claim of "relationship" to Israel until DNA testing was perfected. Testing them in the late 1980s revealed that they not only were related to the Hebrew Nation but they were primarily related to the Tribe of Levi. That would indicate that the rumors and traditions of the Jeremiah group traveling through Arabia and down to Africa might well be history as opposed to rumor.

Is it possible that they took the Ark of the Covenant with them? At this point we can say it is certainly possible. However, the acacia wood that was used to build the ark would have long since disintegrated. The gold leaf that covered it would be left but it would not have the form or the structure of the original ark. The

African Israelis do have their treasures which are only now being revealed, but the ark has not been shared with the public.

5.   RUMORS ABOUT THE LOCATION OF THE ARK

One rumor that persists is that the Ark of the Covenant is currently in Addis-Abba, Ethiopia. The Queen of Sheba was from Ethiopia and the scriptures tell of her visit to Jerusalem during the reign of Solomon. The rumor says that when she returned home she was pregnant with Solomon's son. Years later when that son was grown he went to Jerusalem to visit his father. Before he returned home he stole the Ark of the Covenant from the Temple and that most sacred of religious relics is currently in the Holy of Holies in the Jewish Temple in Addis- Ababa. Is it there? No one knows for sure because the only one allowed to see it is the chief priest and he only enters the Holy of Holies once each year.

True believers tell us that the Ark of the Covenant will turn up when God wills it. It may be hidden in the caves and passageways under the ruins of Solomon's Temple. It may turn up in Babylon (close to Baghdad in Iraq) where it may have been taken at the time of the Babylonian Conquest. It may still be in a cave in the mountains east of the Jordan near where Moses was buried. It may yet turn up as a part of the treasures carried by the Lost Tribe when they went on their pilgrimage to Africa or, in fact, it may be in the temple in Addis-Abba, Ethiopia. To solve this mystery, all of Christendom will have to wait on God's time.

WAS MARK THE GOSPEL WRITER
A DUAL CITIZEN OF ROME AND JERUSALEM?

We first meet Mark in the scriptures when he was a young man living in Jerusalem with his mother, who was identified only as Mary. Her home, which was evidently located somewhere at the edge of Jerusalem, was a frequent meeting place for Jesus and his followers. Mary was most likely a widow since her husband, Mark's father, was never mentioned. Barnabas, a native of Cyprus and identified by Paul as a cousin of Mark's, was evidently sent by the family to help with the care of Mary and the raising of her son. Jewish tradition required that a male member of the family would step in to help if a woman in the family was widowed. If the male member of the family had a brother, that brother was required to marry his brother's widow. This was their way of taking care of the women and children, those least able to take care of themselves, in that male-dominated society.

The young Mark is identified in the scriptures first as John, then as John-Mark, and then only as Mark. He was often identified as being close by the disciples and was present at the Garden of Gethsemane when Jesus was taken by the guards. At that tumultuous time in Mark's life it is likely he was only thirteen or fourteen years of age. Later, Mark became a part of the first missionary journey of Paul and Barnabas, a constant companion of Peter, and then a participant in the missionary work of Paul later in his life.

The question is "Was Mark a dual Hebrew-Roman citizen like Paul?" There is nothing in the scriptures that identifies Mark as a Roman dual citizen but the evidence that he was is significant. There are three items of evidence that can be cited both from the scriptures and from the history of that time that supports the case that Mark was, indeed, a dual Hebrew-Roman citizen:

1. THE NAMES JOHN, JOHN-MARK, AND MARK AS CITED IN THE SCRIPTURES

John is a traditional Hebrew name while Mark (sometimes spelled Marc) is a Roman name. Many males in the Hebrew Nation were named John or some derivative thereof. On the other hand, there are no other Bible characters named Mark, though we find the name Mark all through Roman history. The most notable character in Roman history with that surname is Marc Antony, who was a contemporary of Julius Caesar. He became the leader of Rome's Eastern Legions.

It is unlikely that a Jew would take the name of the hated Romans unless there was some good reason for it. In Mark's case, it is likely that he needed to be identified as a Roman as he reached adulthood if he was to play his role as traveling companion to Peter and writer of the gospel that was planned as an outreach into Greek and Roman society.

2. BECOMING A ROMAN CITIZEN IN THE FIRST CENTURY A.D.

During the lifetime of Mark the Gospel writer and before, there were only two ways to become a Roman citizen: to be born to it and to serve in the Roman Legions. Later, seventy-five to a hundred years following the Crucifixion of Christ when Rome began to decline, Roman citizenship became a commodity that could be purchased by those who found it useful to be Roman citizens. However, during the lifetime of Mark the options for attaining Roman citizenship were limited.

Since Mark could not have been born into Roman citizenship and was just a boy when he first appears in the scriptures, one must speculate about what happened to Mark's father. For that matter, Paul the Apostle also had a missing father and proudly claimed Roman citizenship. It is possible that both had fathers who either volunteered to join the Roman Legions or were conscripted into military service. In either case the soldier and his family would have been given Roman citizenship at the end of his twenty-five-year term of service or if/when he was killed in battle.

It is possible that the fathers of both Paul and Mark were killed in service to the Roman Legions. It is also possible that if one or both volunteered to serve the Romans, they might have been disowned and/or considered dead by their families. During that time in history it was one thing to be under the domination of the hated Romans and quite another to actually choose to join them.

3. TRAVELING FROM PROVINCE TO PROVINCE IN THE ROMAN EMPIRE

The history of the conquests of Alexander the Great and the Romans who followed his decline are both important in the history of the Christian missionary movement. The plan for controlling the various provinces within the Roman Empire included keeping the people of the various units separate from each other to the extent possible. Thus, a person was free to travel or trade only within his own province. He could not cross the border to a neighboring province without being in violation of Roman law. If Paul the Apostle and the young John-Mark were, in fact, both citizens of Rome, it would fit well into the "necessities" of their missionary work. Being citizens they could travel from province to province within the Roman Empire.

Alexander the Great envisioned a great empire where all of the conquered people became citizens of Greece/Macedonia. With that in mind, he forced the Greek model of society on all the territories he conquered. Thus, the population was forced to learn the Greek language and use Greek weights and measures for trading. Alexander established learning centers--colleges/universities and libraries--in all corners of his kingdom where Greek was taught and used. The fact that the Greek language became universal was a major factor in the later missionary effort of the disciples.

In contrast, when the Roman Empire succeeded Alexander's, the Romans envisioned Rome as the center of the world with the conquered countries and people being taxed to the benefit of Rome. They did not want a common language, religion, or trade between the various provinces. Such commonality might be unifying and might inspire the various conquered countries to form alliances to create an uprising against Rome. Rome wanted only two things from their many conquered territories: taxes and peace.

Thus, a Roman citizen could move from province to province, but non-Romans could not. Trade was promoted between Rome and the provinces but not between the individual provinces. The purpose of the Roman Empire was to enrich Rome.

A second factor affected travel from province to province. Because of the Roman domination, a significant number of rebels, zealots, and other disenfranchised people existed in the wilderness areas between the cities. (Scripture records the story of Barabbas and, most likely, Simon the Zealot who followed Jesus, as examples of disenfranchised people.) These people made their living by preying on the trade caravans and other travelers who ventured forth between the various cities. Travel anywhere was dangerous. However, to harm a Roman citizen meant an instant death sentence.

The robbery of non-Roman citizens was generally ignored. Thus, bands of dissidents who made their living as "highway men" avoided travelers who were Roman and focused on non-Roman travelers. It was a crime against Rome to identify yourself as a citizen of Rome when you weren't, but we can imagine that any traveling groups who were Roman would identify themselves as Roman in some significant way to avoid the dangers of being robbed.

The effect on the Christian missionary efforts of the apostles by the two great kingdoms that came into being in the four hundred years before the birth of Christ was two-fold: 1) it provided a common language, Greek; and, 2) what the Romans called *Pax Romana*, or the Roman peace. It was a time when there were no wars in that region for more than three hundred years.

Into this situation came Paul the Apostle who was a Roman citizen and, thus, could travel freely from province to province by virtue of his Roman citizenship. Peter, the other apostle who traveled far and wide, unfortunately, could not. He was Hebrew and Jewish and without major help he could not travel from province to province. Still, the scriptures tell us that Peter traveled from Judea to Syria, up into present-day Turkey and, eventually, to Rome.

If Peter could not move from province to province as a citizen of Judea, how did he manage to travel so far from his roots? The answer may be in his choice of Mark as his traveling companion. Mark may not have had much to offer the older Christian missionary but a major contribution he could make to Peter's travels was, perhaps, his Roman citizenship. If Mark was a citizen of Rome, he could help the Apostle Peter travel with impunity in that time of dangerous travel and Roman domination. Without a companion who had Roman citizenship, Peter would have found it impossible to travel throughout the region and, eventually, to Rome itself. Mark was most likely the necessary ingredient in Peter's missionary journeys.

No other explanation for Peter's relatively free travel across the Roman Empire is mentioned in the scriptures that offers a more viable explanation.

GOD'S PLAN TO SPREAD HIS GOSPEL

William Barkley wrote two wonderful books titled *The Mind of Jesus* and *The Mind of Paul*. In both he attempts to tell us not only what each did during their lifetimes but also what they were thinking and why they did what they did. Obviously, Barkley and other writers have some evidence to work with when they begin such a study of personalities in the Bible. However, no one knows the mind of God Almighty and so whatever is said on the subject is, at best, an educated speculation. So what follows is also an educated speculation.

When you take any part of the scriptures out of context and look at them separately, it is easy to fall into the trap of thinking that the Bible is just a series of unconnected historic happenings. It is natural to wonder what God had in mind as he allowed this 3,000-year odyssey to play out. However, when you look at the Old and New Testaments and read specifically Paul's letters, the overall plan comes into focus.

1.   *Why did God take his chosen people to Egypt and leave them there for 430 years?*

When they went into Egypt, they were nomads and herdsman. When they came out of Egypt all those many years later, they were craftsmen, business men, architects, farmers, hydro-engineers, etc. Many were among the most educated and skilled in Egypt.

2.   *Why did God make his chosen people wander in the wilderness for forty years?*

When they entered the wilderness of Sinai, they had been slaves for several centuries, with a slave servant's mentality. When they emerged from the wilderness and entered Canaan, they were a disciplined military group, hardened by living off of the land and protecting themselves from all of the threats that followed them from Egypt to the Jordan.

3.   *Why is the Holy Land the most conquered country/region in the history of the world?*

As we read the scriptures we see many references to conquering armies and to the influences of the dominant powers in the region. In Biblical times the dominant powers in the Middle East were, in order of emergence, Egypt, Assyria, Babylon, Persia, Greece/Macedonia, and Rome. Unfortunately, Israel fell subject to all of these countries one after the other for over 2,000 years. Each played a role in the development of the Holy Land, the Hebrew Nation, and set the stage for what God had planned for the future.

To understand why the Holy Land was conquered over and over, we have only to look at the map of the region. The dominant countries during that time were located northwest of the Holy Land (Greece and Rome), north (Assyria), east (Babylon and Persia), and south (Egypt). While the dominant countries of the northwest, north, and east changed over the decades and centuries, the one constant was Egypt in the south. Egypt was at the mouth of the Nile, which provided an easy trade route by boat into the interior of Africa. Because of the volatile nature of the Mediterranean Sea that made it impassible much of the year, and the desert to the west of the Holy Land, the trade routes had to pass through the Holy Land. Thus, to reach the riches of Africa, the other dominant countries had to go through that narrow strip of land to reach Egypt and the mouth of the Nile. The country that controlled the trade routes controlled all business and commerce throughout the region.

4.   *Why is Alexander the Great's conquest of the Middle East so important to the overall plan to spread the Gospel?*

God was preparing his missionaries to communicate from Rome to India. Having a common language was an imperative.

The influence of Alexander the Great in the region was major. He conquered the known world from Greece to India and south to Egypt. He brought with him the foremost culture in the world at the time, along with the Greek language and military control. Alexander envisioned one empire with commonality of language and culture from border to border. Thus, the Greek language became the dominant language of the region. Schools were created and Greek was taught in the schools. It became the business transaction language and everyone who was involved in trade or government activities had to know how to communicate in Greek.

The language of the street in Israel was Aramaic, which is considered a "dead" language today. Jesus spoke Aramaic on the streets of Nazareth and Jerusalem. Virtually all Jews spoke at least three languages, Aramaic, Greek, and Hebrew. As is true in many parts of the world today, there is a language of religion, a language of business and education, and a language of the street.

For example, in India today, the language of religion is Hindi, the language of business and education is English, and the language of the street depends on where in India you live. In Mumbai (the British called it Bombay) it is Marathi, the language of the province of Maharashtra. In Calcutta it is Bengali. In Sri Lanka the three languages are Sinhala, English, and Tamile.

It is important to note that there are four important language influences in the scriptures. These are Aramaic, Hebrew, Greek, and Roman/Latin. The Old Testament was written in Hebrew and the New Testament was written in Greek. Alexander the Great had conquered the known world spreading Greek culture and language throughout the region. Greek had become the language of business and education. An educated man like the Apostle Matthew probably could speak at least four languages and, perhaps, others as well.

The Old Testament was written in Hebrew primarily for the Hebrew Nation. No one else was intended to read the scriptures other than the Jews. The New Testament was written with a broader audience in mind. By the time Matthew, Mark, Luke, and John were writing their Gospels and Paul was writing letters to the churches he had created, the group was focused on the Gentiles. Gentiles from the borders of Europe to India all spoke Greek while only the Jews in the Holy Land spoke Hebrew. Thus, Greek was the inclusive language of choice for the New Testament.

5.   Why was the Hebrew Nation's approach to education important in the overall plan to spread the gospel?

It is said that the Greeks were the most educated people in the world at that time in history. History teaches us that they were also the most advanced of all the countries in their culture and politics. They perfected the beginnings of democracy and had a major effect on the world of science, art, and philosophy. However, the Greeks educated only half of their population--the male half.

The Hebrew Nation was created by Moses in the wilderness of Sinai, and he believed that every person--male and female--should be able to read the scriptures. So, Moses and the Hebrew leadership created an educational system that included their female children (the future mothers of their children) as well as the boys.

When Jesus was a boy, tradition tells us, he was educated by his mother. She taught him to read and write and to do the mathematics necessary for the time. At around the age of twelve many of the male children were turned over to their fathers to be educated in the skills necessary to earn a living. Young women continued to learn with their mothers. Young men who showed unusual ability were sent to the rabbi at the Temple in Jerusalem to continue their education. (Indeed, the word *rabbi* in Hebrew means teacher.) Only the very best and brightest progressed to that level. At the Temple, the most learned men studied together and taught the most promising of their young men. Paul the Apostle was one of those young men. He tells us in his letters that he studied under the Rabbi Gamaliel.

We know from reading Luke 2: 40-50 that Jesus created quite a sensation when he visited the Temple in Jerusalem with his parents when he was twelve years of age. They were amazed at his knowledge of the scriptures and his intelligence.

6.   *Why was Rome's conquest of the region important in the overall plan to spread the gospel?*

One of the most outstanding traits of the Romans was their organizational ability. They organized virtually everything from how business and commerce would operate, to a military control system, to holding a census, and setting up a local governance system to function under the supervision of a local Roman governor. They also kept very good written records of the happenings of the time including wars, floods, volcano eruptions, earthquakes, births and deaths, etc. They excelled at many things but were especially good at organizing.

The Romans were primarily interested in two things from the countries they conquered, peace and taxes. They did not want an uprising of the people and they wanted to tax the people of their territories to the maximum so they could take the riches home to Rome.

Conquered countries were divided into manageable units. Borders between countries/territories were controlled. That kept the people from getting together to rebel against the Romans. Roman citizens, on the other hand, could move from place to place with impunity and that is an important factor as it relates to the missionary travels of Peter and Paul.

A Roman citizen was free to travel throughout the empire. During that time in history there were only two ways to become a Roman citizen. One was to be born or adopted into a Roman family and the other was to join the army and fight for Rome. Paul the Apostle told us in his writing that he was a Roman citizen and also was a citizen of Tarsus. The scriptures do not tell us how Paul came to be a Roman citizen but it is likely his father served in the Roman army. Since Paul's father was never mentioned in the scriptures it is likely he was killed. His service would have made his entire family citizens of Rome.

The Gospel writer Mark was originally called John in the scriptures, then John-Mark, then just Mark. John is a Hebrew name. Mark is a Roman name. Like Paul, it is probable that Mark was a dual citizen, though the scriptures do not speak to this issue. His father could have been a Roman soldier who was killed in the service of Rome and that would make Mark a Roman citizen. Mark became the traveling companion of Peter and his dual citizenship may have been the reason Peter chose him. Like Paul, he could have moved through the Roman check points from country to country with impunity.

In summary, when we look at the entire scope of the Bible it is obvious that God had a plan through the centuries to spread his gospel to everyone on earth. That plan included education, language, business practices, conquests, and exile. Each happening made a unique contribution to the overall plan. It is important to realize that the plan is still underway today and we are a part of it.

THE CONTRIBUTIONS OF PAUL THE APOSTLE

Paul the Apostle contributed thirteen letters to the content of the New Testament. It is likely that Paul wrote many other letters that we do not have copies of to include in our Holy Bible. Only Luke contributed more in volume to the New Testament than Paul.

It should not be a surprise that Paul also contributed more controversy than any other writer. Many of the letters Paul wrote seemed to be in conflict with each other and there is good reason for that. Paul was a prolific letter writer. He had months and years of time on his hands moving from prison to prison, from Philippi to Caesarea by the Sea to Rome, and other possible prison locations we may not know of. He may have written several hundred letters during his thirty-plus-year ministry. He would probably have been surprised to find that thirteen of his letters, some written years apart and some with possible contradictions, are now included side by side in the New Testament.

WHO WAS PAUL?

Paul of Tarsus was named Saul at his birth, most likely after Israel's first king who was the original mentor and benefactor of King David. Like King Saul, Paul was a member of the tribe of Benjamin. His dual names Saul and Paul could be accounted for like John-Mark's names. Saul was a name of Jewish tradition while Paul came from his birth into a family where they had both Hebrew and Roman citizenship. Paul was a Roman name. That fact would affect virtually everything Paul did throughout his Christian ministry.

At the time Paul was born, his home town was neither a Jewish nor a Roman city though properties of both were present. It was one of the cities conquered and "recreated" by Alexander the Great and though it remained an Asian-influenced city, it had many of the characteristics of the cities of Greece. The Greek language was spoken there and Greek literature and culture were the standards. This accounts for the fact that Paul was fluent in the Greek language and it made him at home in his travels throughout the Asian, Macedonian, and Greek countryside where virtually everyone could speak Greek.

Paul was a tent-maker by trade and it is customary to learn your trade from your father, though Paul's father is never mentioned in the scriptures. Tarsus was the right place to live if you were a tent-maker because as a city it was well known for the coarse goat's hair cloth called *cilicia* that was used to make tents, sails, awnings, and cloaks. This tent-maker's skill gave Paul financial independence during his many travels.

Paul was a well-educated young man. Though born and raised in Tarsus, he was educated in Jerusalem from about the age of fifteen. He studied under Gamaliel, one of the best known *rabbis* or teachers of that time. In many ways Paul and Jesus were contemporaries and about the same age, with one studying the scriptures in Nazareth and the other studying in Jerusalem.

Saul-Paul appears first in the scriptures at the stoning of Stephen. (Acts 13:16-61) He did not participate in the stoning but was identified as a witness, where the others . . .

"...laid their clothes at the feet of a young man called Saul." (Acts 13: 58)

WHAT DID PAUL DO?

Paul is given rightful credit for being the first missionary and his purpose was to win the lost to Christ and to create churches for the development and nurturing of both Christianity and the new converts to the faith.

Paul made four pilgrimages recorded in the scriptures. He went first to the central area of present day Turkey, then twice he traveled to Macedonia and Greece. The last missionary journey he traveled to

Rome as prisoner of the Romans who took him there to be tried before the Roman leadership. Some scholars believe that Paul was found innocent and released after his trial in Rome and returned to Ephesus. They believe he was then arrested again during the major persecution that followed the burning of Rome by the Emperor Nero in 63 A.D. and taken to Rome a second time where he met his demise. Thus, he may have had five pilgrimages. However, there is no scripture to support this latter journey to Rome.

During Paul's missionary journeys he set up at least a dozen churches and possibly many more. We have a record only of those listed in his letters and in the Book of Acts. Paul also wrote many letters designed to help the pastors and members of the churches with their organization and to solve problems. In Paul's letters we find the foundations of church organization, qualifications of pastors and deacons, rules for church conduct, and many other things that remain a part of our church tradition today.

WHEN DID PAUL SERVE?

Paul's conversion was on the road to Damascus while he was attempting to carry out the will of the Pharisee leadership in persecuting the Christians. This probably occurred about one year after the Resurrection and Ascension of Christ. Paul then remained in the service of Jesus until around 65 A.D. when he was most likely put to death in Rome following his captivity there. Thus, Paul had a ministry that spanned more than three decades. Only John, Timothy, and Mark may have served Christ longer.

WHY DID PAUL BECOME AN APOSTLE?

It is an amazing attribute of Jesus to choose what seemed to be just normal, average men to provide the necessities of the beginnings of Christianity and then to turn them into strong and dynamic ministers and missionaries for His service. It is still happening today.

Paul was well educated, a strong-willed person, knowledgeable in the teachings and ways of the Pharisees, financially independent with a marketable trade, and he was a Roman citizen. All of these translated into the longest and most dynamic impact on Christianity in its infancy and Christianity today. Except for Jesus, no person exceeded Paul's impact on the early and present church.

WHERE DID PAUL LIVE?

Paul was born and spent his early life in Tarsus, a Greek/Roman city located at the border of present-day Turkey and the northern section of the Holy Land. He spent his years between the ages of fifteen and twenty-five studying in Jerusalem. Following that time in his life, Paul never again had a home base. He traveled the known world sharing the gospel with all who would listen and his last trip took him to the center of the Roman Empire.

PAUL'S MAJOR CONTRIBUTIONS

When Jesus left this earth, Christianity did not have...

1. members anyplace in the world other than Israel;

2. missionaries to spread the word of Jesus Christ, the Messiah;

3. the implementation of the New Testament as a New Covenant between God and His people;

4. churches, nor the knowledge of how to organize a church;

5. pastors of churches, nor the knowledge of what a pastor should do;

6. deacons as a part of a church organization, nor the knowledge of what deacons should do;

7. or group benevolences such as caring for the poor and the widows.

Forty years after Paul met Jesus on that road to Damascus, Christianity had all of the above and more, plus there were Christians from India to Greece, and from South Central Asia to Southern Europe. Such was Paul's impact on Christianity and the history of the world.

History has many pairings of people that had significant effects on the lives and times in which they lived. In each case there was a thinker/philosopher and a more pragmatic follower who put the thoughts of the philosopher into practice.

In ancient Greece there was Socrates the philosopher and his student Plato, who wrote the rudiments of democracy that came from his teacher/philosopher.

At the beginning of the United States the revolutionary philosophy of the republic form of government came from the minds of John Adams, Benjamin Franklin, and Thomas Jefferson, but the pragmatic expression of that philosophy came with the presidency of George Washington.

During the 1960s there was the U.S. presidency of John F. Kennedy where many new social programs were authored. Former Vice President Lyndon Johnson followed Kennedy into the office of the president with the practical know-how to get revisions to the Social Security program and to put many of the new programs into law, including both Medicare and Medicaid.

Jesus and Paul had such a relationship. Jesus gave the example to live by and the philosophy of relationships that made each person his "brother's keeper." Paul followed with his Pharisee training and his foundational understanding of how organizations work and how to plan for the establishment, organization, and expansion of Christianity. These understandings and skills were combined in a person who was described as zealous. He was a man with a strong spirit, the ability to put his skills to work, and a purpose that was bigger than himself and beneficial to all mankind. What more could one ask?

THE DEVELOPMENT OF PAUL, THE THEOLOGIAN AND LEADER

As you read the letters of Paul the Apostle, remember that he was going through a developmental process just like any other minister or missionary. He was raised a Jew. He studied under Gamaliel, one of the greatest rabbis of his day, to become a Pharisee and he moved into that Jewish religious leadership group at around the age of twenty-five. He was, by nature, a hard-working and persistent person. Whatever he did he put his whole self into it. By his nature we can assume that he was a very well-studied and devout Jew.

After meeting Jesus on the road to Damascus, he became a Christian with all of the training and understandings of a Jew, but with none of the developmental background of the disciples. He had not listened to Jesus preach. He had not had the opportunity to talk to Jesus and ask Him the questions that would have been troubling to anyone of that time. He was, in every sense of the word, learning as he traveled and as he faced the many challenges that were a part of the day- to-day life of a new minister. At the same time he was trying to create both knowledge and understanding in his people, he was working to create that same knowledge and understanding within himself as he grew day by day. He wasn't a finished product and, as he confessed over and over in his letters, he ran his race the best he could but never reached "perfection."

JESUS FOR THE JEWS

Paul believed Jesus was the promised Messiah and he knew that the Messiah had been promised to the Jews. He saw his first responsibility as presenting Jesus to the Jewish leadership and striving to see that Jesus was not rejected by the Jews. Failing that, he had to redirect his effort to the Gentiles and that was, obviously, a very difficult decision for him.

In reading the thirteen letters Paul wrote to the churches and his pastor friends, we can feel Paul leaning on his training as a Pharisee. As the years passed, he realized that he was not going to be successful in restructuring Judaism from the inside. He came to the realization that he was, in actuality, helping to create an entirely new religious order. Thus, his directions to the Christian churches became more liberal and more inclusive. As an example, in the early years he obviously assumed that men would provide the leadership for the family and for the church as was true in the structure of Judaism. Later, you could read his admonition that

> *There is no Jew or Greek, slave or free, male or female; for you are all one in Christ Jesus. (Galatians 3: 28)*

In a very real sense he evolved to the point where he helped to create the foundation for equality between people whatever their station, their religion, or their gender. He helped to create the foundations of democracy as it is practiced today. At that time in history the "equality" position was revolutionary and it was especially so for a person who had been raised as a Jew and trained into the Jewish leadership.

PAUL AND CONTROVERSY

When we study the scriptures, nothing is more frustrating than to read something in one place that seems to instruct us one way only to read something in another location that points us in an entirely different direction. The frustration is doubly troubling when the same writer does that in different scriptures, as Paul's letters seem to do in several places. However, to understand Paul's writing we must place ourselves in the context of Paul's situation. In short, the reader must realize that Paul is...

1. in development himself even as he attempts to help the churches with their problems;

2. sometimes writing in broad general principles for the instruction of all and sometimes he is writing in specifics to deal with short-term problems presented to him by individual churches. Most of the time his directions are consistent but sometimes specific problems require specific remedies that are not consistent with the more general principles stated elsewhere;

3. limited in his responses to the available solutions. As new solutions are presented in subsequent centuries, Paul might have chosen a different response. For example, because wine seemed to be the best solution for a stomach problem in Paul's day, it does not mean that we should use wine today to solve that problem and not use other remedies as they are made available to us.

PAUL AND THE DOCTRINE OF INERRANCY

Most find it easy to justify the doctrine of "inerrancy" as it relates to the original scriptures. God ordained that the Bible would be written by men inspired by the Spirit of God. Those who wrote the Bible wrote it in their own language and in the context of their time. However, the Bible has changed in language and presentation since it was written. The following outline gives a perspective of the "how" and "why" of the changes.

A. God inspired his followers to write the scriptures from Genesis to Revelation and man wrote as God directed.

B. Man then attempted to perpetuate the scriptures and to translate them so they could be shared worldwide.

1. Man copied the scriptures to preserve them.

2. Man translated the scriptures to share them with those of other languages:

    a. Hebrew to Greek

    b. Hebrew and Greek to Latin Vulgate

    c. Greek to Old English

    d. Old English to New English

    e. Revised into modern "meaning" English

    f. Revised again, and then again

In every place where man attempted to copy or translate the scriptures there is opportunity for error or, at least, for misdirection.

One of the key examples that causes confusion and, in history, caused much debate and consternation among many Christians over the years relates to how man shall find his salvation. Some have justified their prejudices by taking individual scriptures out of context and using them to justify a particular perspective. Note the following:

Paul: Man finds his salvation through faith.

By grace are ye saved through faith, it is the gift of God, not of works lest any man should boast. (Ephesians 2: 8)

James: Man finds his salvation through works.

Ye see then how that by works a man is justified…(James 2: 24)

John: Man finds his salvation through belief.

For God so loved the world that He gave His only begotten son, that whosoever believeth in Him shall not perish but have ever lasting life. (John 3: 16)

Mark: Man finds his salvation through belief and baptism.

Whoever believes and is baptized will be saved, but whoever does not believe will be condemned. (Mark 16: 16)

None of the scriptures above are intended to be mutually exclusive. God gave mankind the scriptures in total and did not intend for them to be separated from the text and used out of context. One can justify the statement that God intended for the reader to be saved through believing in God, having faith in God's will and direction, and that the in-dwelling spirit of a person's salvation would cause each person to want to be baptized into a Christian fellowship. Then, the combination of all three would promote good works from each person toward their fellow man.

PAUL AND HIS WRITING ABOUT WOMEN AND THEIR PLACE IN THE CHURCH AND IN SOCIETY

Of all the possible contradictions in Paul's letters, none has caused more discussion and confusion than his seeming relegation of women to second-class citizens in the church.

In the 1st Corinthians, Paul answers a query from the leadership of the church in Corinth by telling them

"Let the women keep silent in the churches…" (1st Corinthians 14: 34)

We don't know what the query was to which Paul was responding. We can surmise that Paul had been told of a situation where one or more women in the church were calling attention to themselves and, perhaps, were dominating the discussions and creating dissension among the members. Some have suggested that in a city where prostitution was a major way of life, some of the women may have attempted to ply their trade in virtually any gathering where men came together, including church gatherings. In this situation Paul, reverting to his Pharisee training, may well have not wanted to exclude them but, instead, may have simply said that these women *"…should keep silent in the church." (1st Corinthians 14: 34)*

That should not negate the more general principle that Paul had presented to the Galatians that stated

There is no Jew or Greek, slave or free, male or female; for you are all one in Christ Jesus. (Galatians 3:28)

The "keep silent" directive is, obviously, a response to a specific query while the "neither male nor female" comment is the general principle we should follow in our relationships and in organizing our churches. Equality is the principle and the intent but sometimes, to solve a short-range problem, one needs to use the "equality" with good sense.

In another location in the Bible, Paul was dealing with the issue of marriage and told the reader that

It is better to be as I am" [meaning celibate and unmarried] *but if they do not have self control, they should marry, for it is better to marry than to burn with desire. (1ˢᵗ Corinthians 7:9)*

Obviously, Paul is not against the institution of marriage. In the ministry of Jesus, two institutions were ordained, the church and the family. Without marriage the second of these could not be. Thus, Paul is talking about the obvious fact that being "unfettered" from domestic responsibilities allowed him to conduct his ministry more completely and with total devotion and focus. He was talking to the pastors of churches and not to the general population.

In other places in Paul's letters he was, obviously, responding to specific requests for help in dealing with problems in the various churches. In one place he stated

"I do not allow a woman to teach or to have authority over a man ..." *(1ˢᵗ Timothy 2: 12)*

Imagine in that context that Paul had been told of a situation where he had previously preached to a congregation and given specific instructions to the male leadership. Then, later, he was told that women whom he had not "trained" for leadership were beginning to direct the group regarding the new gospel. Paul might have simply told them to stop giving instruction to the men. Now take some license and add the words "to the men whom I have trained." Both God and Paul placed women in authority over men in other circumstances and in other times. The list of women includes Phobe (Romans), Priscilla (Acts), Deborah (Judges) and many others.

Perhaps the most difficult scripture to deal with in the King James Bible, written in English, is the specific admonition from Paul that said...

"... The husband is head of the wife as Christ is Head of the church. (1ˢᵗ Cor. 11: 3)

To deal with the intent of this sentence one has to compare the English words with the original Greek. In English, the word "head" means, literally, the physical head of one's body and, figuratively, the leader of a body of people. The two meanings are intertwined. That is not so in Greek. There are two words that are used to mean head. Those words are *arche* (pronounced ar-KAY) and *kaphale* (pronounced kef-ah-LAY).

The word *arche* is used in the Greek language to mean "first." It is sometimes translated to mean magistrate, chief, prince, ruler, head, etc. The word *kaphale* means "foremost" or "to lead out." A *kephale* was one who went before the troops, the leader in the sense of being in the lead, the first one into battle. Thus, one word (*arche*) means "boss" and the other (*kephale*) means "first one into battle" or "protector of the family."

Had Paul written that the husband is the *arche* (head) of the wife, he would have meant that the husband was to rule over the wife. However, he wrote that the husband is the *kephale* of the wife. Thus, Paul obviously intended that the husband was to be the protector of the wife, to lead as the first line of defense when there is trouble or difficulty.

Paul was raised using the Greek language. His native Tarsus was a Greek/Roman city and so the language was not a "second" language to him, it was his native language. Had he intended to use the word *arche* and meant for the husband to be the boss, the ruler, the leader of the wife, he would have said it. Instead, he took great care not to say that. He used the word *kephale* and his meaning is obvious. He meant that the husband should be the protector of the wife and family.

Jesus was never quoted by any of the writers of the gospels as saying that man was to rule over woman. Women were used by both Jesus and Paul in leadership positions, often ministering and providing leadership in a variety of situations. Thus, if we go back to the original Greek, as the inspired writer Paul wrote it, the intent was never that man should be the ruler and woman to be the subject. One might ask, "How then shall we live together as man and wife? Who is the boss?"

If married couples are honest with each other, they would confess that each partner provides leadership in a variety of different areas. Shakespeare said, "All of the world is a stage and the people merely players, and in life each person plays many roles." We could say the same thing about marriage. We all play many roles. Who is dominant? Who is subject? Most likely each partner has staked out leadership and "follow-ship" roles over the years and no one partner provides leadership in all areas of the relationship.

That situation plays out in our churches as well. All churches are organized with various areas of leadership. The key question to struggle with is "Which positions in the church are the most important?" Did Jesus or Paul say that one was more important than another? There is no scripture that indicates that one job in a church is more important than another.

There are many other examples to "explain" Paul's writings. However, suffice it to say that Paul wrote both in broad philosophical approaches and also for the purpose of problem solving related to specific questions. Most of the time both of these approaches were consistent but sometimes solving the problems of individual congregations required measures that were not completely consistent with the philosophical principles that he espoused for the broader Christian community.

Note: The information related to translation of the Greek language into English came from a book titled What Paul Really Said About Women by John T. Bristow (HarperOne, 1991). Additional information was received from Dr. Bryan Bibb, who teaches Hebrew at Furman University, and Dr. Randal Ruble, long-time teacher of Hebrew and Biblical Studies in the seminary at Erskine College.

THE TREATMENT OF WOMEN IN THE BIBLE

There are times when the old rhythm jingle "The Bible says it, I believe it, and that settles it," works just fine. It is comforting to be able to read the Bible and take, literally, what it says. Unfortunately, as the Bible relates to the life, contribution, and role of women, that simple approach just doesn't suffice. It is all much more complicated than that. Perhaps some of what follows will clarify.

The following four verses all appear in scriptures credited to the Apostle Paul and have been used for centuries to justify the second-class citizenship of women both in the church and in society.

Wives submit to your husbands as to the Lord. For the husband is the head of the wife as Christ is the head of the church,...(Ephesians 5: 22-24)

But I want you to know that Christ is the head of every man, and the man is the head of the woman, and God is the head of Christ. (1st Corinthians 11:3)

The women should be silent in the churches, for they are not permitted to speak, but should be submissive, as the law also says. And, if they want to learn something, they should ask their own husbands at home, for it is disgraceful for a woman to speak in the church meeting. (1ˢᵗ Corinthians 14: 34-35)

A women should learn in silence with full submission. I do not allow a women to teach or have authority over a man: Instead, she is to be silent. (1ˢᵗ Timothy 2: 11)

Let's deal first with the issue of translation.

TRANSLATION OF SCRIPTURE

In English, the word "head" means, literally, the physical head of one's body and/or the leader of a body of people. The two meanings are intertwined. That is not so, however, in Greek where two different and distinct words are translated as "head." One of these words is *arche* (pronounced ar-KAY). It means head in terms of leadership or point of origin. The Greek language used this word as a prefix for words including archaeology and archetype, both relating to first things. *Arche* was also used to designate first in importance and power such as in archangel, archbishop, and archduke. All relate to the head of a group in terms of leadership. In the original Greek written in the New Testament, including the letters written by Paul, the word *arche* was used also for such meanings as magistrate, chief, prince, ruler, head, and so forth.

As regards the issue with whether or not husbands should command their wives and rule over them, Paul could have written that the husband is the *arche* (head) of the wife. He would have meant that the husband is to rule over the wife. However, Paul did not choose to use the word *arche* when he wrote of how the husband is head of his wife. Instead, he used the word *kephale* (pronounced kef-ah-LAY). This word does mean "head" as in the part of one's body. It was also used to mean "head" as in fore or foremost. This word was never used to mean "leader" or "boss" or "chief" or "ruler." *Kephale* was often used as a military term as in "one who goes before the troops, the first one into battle." In a sense it means "protector" since the one who goes first is the first line of defense and the protector of his troops or of his family.

So, who translated this scriptural word in such a way that we missed what Paul was trying to tell us? The answer is the English did it when they created the King James Bible. Before we are too harsh on them, we should remember that most women were considered to be property at the time, to be bought and sold. Who would not read such a scripture and think that Paul was stating the obvious with what he was writing? Men were the leaders, the head of women. Why would they even have questioned it?

It is unfortunate that when an English-speaking person reads that "the husband is head of his wife" that he will normally conclude that this means the husband is to rule over his wife. However, Paul deliberately chose the other word. People who depend on the English translation cannot know that Paul's word was not *arche* but *kephale*. Thus, Paul was telling us that the husband was the "protector" of his wife and family, not the ruler over his wife and family.

If one looks at the Hebrew language for the word meaning "physical head" or "ruler" in the Old Testament, the word is *rosh*. Those who were responsible for writing and perpetuating the Hebrew Bible were very careful about the use of the word.

WOMEN LEADERS APPOINTED BY GOD

One can make the case that all women, wherever their lives were chronicled in the Bible, were appointed by God. However, for purposes of this discussion they are broken into three groups: Old Testament leaders, associates of Jesus, and associates of Paul the Apostle.

Old Testament Leaders:

<u>Deborah:</u> She was a prophet, judge, and a warrior leader of the Hebrew Nation against the Canaanites. She was also a wife and mother but that did not keep God from placing her in command of the Hebrew army at a crucial time in their history. You can read about her in the Book of Judges, Chapters 4 and 5.

<u>Esther:</u> She was an unwitting Biblical leader, but an incredibly brave and wise one nonetheless. She defied her husband, saved her people, and won concessions for the treatment of the Hebrew slaves who were in exile in Persia. You can read her story in the Book of Esther.

<u>Mary, the Mother of Jesus:</u> God selected Mary to be the mother of our Savior. In effect, God partnered with a woman to bring His son into the world to give us an example to follow. He could have chosen to bring Jesus to the world as a full-grown man ready to minister to the people. Instead, he chose to bring Jesus to earth as a baby so he would, indeed, be both God and man. You can read the story of the birth of Jesus in the Gospels of Matthew and Luke.

Associates of Jesus:

<u>Martha:</u> She was one of Jesus' closest friends and disciples. According to the Gospels of Luke, and John, she opened her home to Him, shared meals with Him, and stood by His side as He raised her brother, Lazarus, from the dead. The gospel of John reports that *"Jesus loved Martha and her sister and Lazarus." (John 11:5).*

<u>Mary Magdalene:</u> Mary seemed to always be at Jesus' side as He traveled and ministered to His disciples and the people. She was at the Last Supper. She was present at His death on the cross. She was among the first witnesses of the empty tomb. Only, perhaps, John

and Peter were closer to Jesus, personally, than Mary Magdalene. Her name is included among the closest associates of Jesus as reported in the Gospels of Matthew, Mark, Luke and John.

Other Women of Note: When referring to the earliest followers of Jesus, the Gospel writers often speak of two groups of disciples, the Twelve and the Women. The Twelve refer to the twelve Jewish men chosen by Jesus to be His closest companions and first apostles, symbolic of the twelve tribes of Israel. The Women refer to an unspecified number of female disciples who also followed Jesus, welcoming Him into their homes, financing His ministry, and often teaching the Twelve through their acts of faithfulness and love. Just as Jesus predicted, most of the Twelve abandoned Him at His death (John 16: 32). But the women remained by His side, through His death, burial, and Resurrection.

Associates of Paul the Apostle:

Tabitha: She was a stalwart force in the first century, working with widows and orphans in Joppa. When she died, God and Peter raised her from the dead (Acts 9: 40). She was the only woman in the New Testament identified with the feminine form of the word disciple, *matheria*.

Junia: Paul wrote in Romans 16:7, *"My fellow Jews who have been in prison with me. They are outstanding among the apostles, and they were in Christ before I was."* She is the first and only woman in scripture to be explicitly identified as an apostle.

Phoebe: Paul said of Phoebe in his letter introducing her to the Romans, *"I commend to you our sister Phoebe, a deacon in the church of Cenchreae. She has been the benefactor of many people including me."* She is identified as a deacon and also a teacher and leader in the church. (The word "deaconess" is a word we made up much later.)

Priscilla: The wife of Aquilla, they both worked with Paul in Corinth to set up the church there. Paul took them with him on a mission trip across to Asia Minor and left them in Ephesus so they could minister to the church there. She is identified as a missionary and a teacher, most specifically as a teacher of Apollos, a learned man who became a significant preacher of the time. Note that she is identified by Paul as teaching a man who became a power in the ministry.

There are many more women who served God, Jesus, and Paul throughout the scriptures that are not mentioned in this text. There were warriors, ministers, prophets, and teachers and even one who served as Queen of Judah. Many of these women are in the following list:

Abigail: Wife of David when he became king of Israel. (1ˢᵗ Samuel: 27: 3)

Abishag: Beautiful young lady who became a caretaker for King David in his later years. (1ˢᵗ Kings 1: 1-4)

Ahinoam: Wife of King David and mother of his oldest son, Amnon. (2ⁿᵈ Samuel 3: 2:1; Chronicles 3: 1)

Anna: A prophetess in Jerusalem who heralded the young Jesus when He was brought to the Temple for the first time. (Luke 2: 32-38)

Asenath: Egyptian wife of Joseph who was the mother of Manasseh and Eplraim. (Genesis 46: 21)

Athaliah: Wife of King Jehoram of Judah. The only ruling queen in Judah's history, she followed Jehoram as ruler from 841-835 B.C. (2ⁿᵈ Kings 11: 2; Chronicles 22-23)

Bathsheba: Her adultery with King David is a well-known story. Her major contribution was as the mother of King Solomon and insuring that he followed David as king. (2ⁿᵈ Samuel 5: 14; 1 Chronicles 14: 4; 1ˢᵗ Kings 1)

Bernice: Eldest daughter of Herod Agrippa. Attempted to save the Temple from destruction by the Romans during the uprising of 67-73 A.D. (Acts 25: 13, 23; 26: 30)

Claudia: A devout Christian woman referred to by Paul in Timothy. (2ⁿᵈ Timothy 4: 21)

Elizabeth: A godly woman who was the mother of John the Baptist and a relative of Mary, the mother of Jesus. (Luke 1: 13-17)

Eunice: Mother of Timothy and a Jewish Christian who hosted Paul and Barnabas in Lystra on their first missionary journey and Paul and Silas on their second. (2ⁿᵈ Timothy 1: 5; 2ⁿᵈ Timothy 3: 15)

Hagar: Egyptian handmaid of Sarah, the wife of Abraham. She became Abraham's second wife at the insistence of Sarah and birthed Abraham's first son, Ishmael. Thus, she is the mother of the Islamic nation as was promised by God. (Genesis 16, 21; Galatians 4: 24)

Hephzibah: Mother of Manasseh, King of Judah. (2nd Kings 21:1)

Huldah: Prophetess in Jerusalem, a contemporary of both Jeremiah and Zephaniah in Jerusalem. 2nd Kings 22: 14; 2nd Chronicles 34: 22)

Jediadah: The wife of King Amon of Judah and the mother of King Josiah, who was known as the "good king" of Judah. (2nd Kings 22: 1)

Leah: She was the daughter of Leban, the wife of Jacob, and the older sister of Rachel. She was mother of two of Jacob's twelve sons. (Genesis 27: 17-18)

Lydia: A Gentile woman converted by Paul in Philippi. She hosted Paul and Silas while they were in Philippi. (Acts 16: 14, 40)

Mary: She was the mother of Mark the Gospel writer who opened her home to the followers of Jesus during his time in Jerusalem. (Acts 12: 12) Note: There were five followers of Jesus named Mary. See Mary the mother of Jesus and Mary Magdalene above.

Miriam: A sister of Moses and Aaron. She was the young girl charged with the task of watching her infant brother's cradle hidden in the reeds of the Nile River. She was later identified as a prophetess and a leader of the nation of Israel. (Exodus 15-20; Numbers 26: 59; Chronicles 6: 3)

Naomi: She was the mother-in-law of Ruth and the subject of some of the best, most loving of all scripture in the Bible. (Ruth 1: 1-2, 20-22)

Nympha: A Christian woman living in Laodicea (or perhaps Colossae) who, at great risk to herself, provided her house for believers to gather for worship. Paul sent greetings to her and the church. (Colossians 4: 15)

Queen of Sheba: An associate of Solomon's who visited him in Jerusalem. Tradition says that she bore Solomon a son and her descendants may, today, be the protectors of the Ark of the Covenant. (1st Kings 10: 1-13; 2nd Chronicles 9: 1-12)

Rachael: Daughter of Leban and second wife of Jacob. She was the mother of Joseph and Benjamin, both patriarchs of the Twelve Tribes of Israel. It was Jacob's love of Rachel that bound him to the family of Leban. (Genesis 29: 10)

Rahab: Heroine of the battle of Jericho. She provided information to the spies sent into Jericho by Joshua and protected them from discovery. She was granted the lives of herself and her family and they became a part of the Hebrew Nation. (John 2-6; 2-11)

Rebekah: The wife of the patriarch Isaac and mother of Jacob and Esau. Laban, who played a dominant role in the life of Jacob, was her brother. (Genesis 24-27; Romans 9: 10)

Ruth: Daughter-in-law of Naomi who stayed with Naomi in an expression of love. She became the wife of Boaz and was in the genealogy line with King David and Jesus. (Book of Ruth)

Salome: A follower of Jesus who was included in the group that he referred to as "the Women." She may have been the sister of Mary the mother of Jesus and also may have been the mother of the disciples James and John. She traveled with the disciples and stood at the foot of the cross at the crucifixion. (Mark 15: 40; Matthew 27: 56)

Sarah: She was the wife of Abraham and her name was originally Sarai. Sarah was the mother of Isaac and, as such, she was the matriarch of the Hebrew Nation. (Genesis 11; 29; 17: 15-16)

Syntyche: She worked with Paul in proclaiming the gospel and evidently held a position of leadership in the Philippian church. (Philippians 4: 2)

Tamar: Her name is recorded in the genealogy of Christ. She was the wife of Er, the first-born son of Judah by a Canaanite. Later, as a widow, Tamar preserved the line of Judah through Perez by bearing him two sons named Perez and Zerah. (Genesis 38: 6-24; Matthew 1: 3)

Typhena: A Christian woman of Rome. Paul called her one of the "Lord's workers." (Romans 16: 12)

<u>Ipporah:</u> The wife of Moses and mother of his sons, Gershom and Eliezer. There is evidence to support that Zipporah accompanied Moses back to Egypt but when trouble started she and the two sons went back to live with her father, Reuel. (Exodus 2: 21; 4: 25)

POSSIBLE MEANINGS OF CONTROVERSIAL VERSES FROM PAUL'S LETTERS

Did Paul the Apostle believe women were second-class citizens? There is strong evidence to the contrary. Note Paul's words in his letter to the Galatians:

There is neither Jew nor Greek, there is neither slave nor free man, there is neither male nor female: for you are all one in Christ Jesus. (Galatians 3: 28)

Most would judge these words to be a general philosophy expressed by Jesus and put into print by Paul. It is a principle for us to follow in our relationships. Considering this philosophy, how could Paul tell women to "keep silent in church" or that "the husband is the head of the wife" or "go home and ask your husbands" if, in fact, all are one (equal) in Christ Jesus?

The answer to that question is related to the fact that Paul possibly wrote as many as several hundred letters over his twenty-five-year ministry. We have only thirteen of them. In ten of the letters he is responding to questions that came from the churches, trying to help them solve their problems. The problems are different from church to church and even different in the same church at different times.

Stop for a minute, re-read Paul's scriptures related to the status of women, and try to formulate the questions that Paul was attempting to answer.

We have already identified the issue of translation, specifically related to the word "head." The following focuses on other such issues.

One explanation worthy of note relates to the admonition to "Keep quiet in church." That was written during a time in history when women outnumbered men in most cities of the Roman Empire two to one. The Roman Legions and the constant border wars took a great toll on the number of men available to become husbands throughout the empire. Also, there were a great many widows who, because of the laws and traditions of the times, could not own property, run a business, or work for the government. The average age at death for a women during that time in history was less than forty. That meant that there were many women who were young and vital widows seeking husbands. Further, because of the impossibility of making a living doing anything legitimate, many were forced into prostitution, which was not illegal in the Roman Empire. To ply their trade, they frequented any gathering where men were present, including church services. Imagine a question to Paul from the leadership of the church at Corinth that said the following:

"We have many women who are attending our church services who continually call attention to themselves in various ways. They are dominating our discussion time and they, obviously, have little to contribute to the discussion. We don't want to exclude them from the services but we need to better control the situation. What would you suggest?"

Paul's answer that they should *"Let the women keep silent in the churches,"* would not seem out of line. Note that he didn't say the same thing to the church at Philippi or Ephesus, just to the one at Corinth where women calling attention to themselves was obviously a problem.

SUMMARY

It is easy to profess that "I believe in the inspired word of God." The "word" as we read it in our English translation Bibles, however, requires further study and evaluation. Seminaries teach both Greek and Hebrew to ministers in training. They believe that the only way you can fully understand the scriptures is to have a thorough knowledge of the language in which the scriptures were written as well as an understanding of the context of the scriptures. There is always the necessity to understand not only what is said but also who is saying it, to whom, and why. Only when you have mastered all four of these necessities can you understand the full meaning of the scriptures and their glorious message to mankind.

God used women in a variety of capacities to further his kingdom here on earth. They were leaders, warriors, judges, and teachers as well as housewives and mothers. God could have chosen to present His son fully grown and ready to minister to the people in the Holy Land. Instead, He chose to bring His Son to earth by partnering with a woman to give birth in the traditional manner so He would, indeed, be considered both God and man.

Jesus treated women with respect and never as second-class citizens. We can read the red letters in the Bible where Jesus is quoted directly and there are no verses that can be misconstrued as demeaning to women or treating them with less status than men.

Paul gets the blame for many of the controversial issues related to the status of women in the Bible. Some of those we can credit to translation of the scriptures from Greek to English and others we can attribute to his attempt to respond to the questions of the various churches as they tried to solve specific problems brought on by the status of women at that time in history. For every verse that Paul wrote that seems to place women in a subservient role, there are dozens that treat women as the equals of men in every way. His most telling philosophy in scripture form regarding the status of women was in Galatians

"There is neither Jew nor Greek, there is neither slave nor free, there is neither male nor female; for you are all one in Christ Jesus. (Galatians 3:28)

A FINAL NOTE FROM THE AUTHOR

No one understands everything in the Bible. I can profess that I believe the Bible from Genesis to maps but readily say that I don't understand everything I read. When I run across something that I don't understand or that does not make sense to me, I generally assume it is because I have not yet studied enough for full understanding.

The verses in the scriptures attributed to Paul the Apostle that seem to designate women as second-class citizens are scriptures that do not make sense to me if taken verbatim and lifted out of the scriptures to stand alone. Not only do they seem inconsistent with other scriptures but they are not consistent with the way Jesus treated women and the roles God gave to women throughout the Old and New Testaments. Further, these scriptures fly in the face of reality as we know it today. Women play leadership roles in all areas of society today as they have throughout history. Contributions of women are many and varied but easily identifiable as adding to the quality of life and as furthering the Kingdom of God. To think otherwise is just not consistent with the scriptures taken in their totality and the living example of Jesus as He walked among us.

THE MYSTERIES SURROUNDING THE BIRTH OF THE CHRIST CHILD

The story of the birth of Christ is probably among the best known scriptures in the Bible. It is the opening story of the New Testament, God's New Covenant with His people. Virtually all Christian faiths believe in 1) the virgin birth, 2) a sacrificial death on a cross, and 3) Christ risen from the dead. The story of the birth of Christ includes shepherds, wise men from the east, and a mysterious star that guided them to Bethlehem of Judea, the birthplace of the promised Messiah. Thus, the circumstances surrounding the birth of Christ form a major part of the Christian's belief system and heritage.

SHEPHERDS IN THE HILLS

The Christmas story as recorded by Luke tells us that there were shepherds in the hills close to Bethlehem keeping watch over their flocks.

In the same region, there were shepherds out in the field keeping watch over their flock by night. And an angel of the Lord appeared to them, and the glory of the Lord shone around them, and they were filled with fear. And the angel said to them, "Be not afraid; for behold, I bring you good news of a great joy which will come to all the people; for to you is born this day in the city of David a Savior, who is Christ the Lord. And this will be a sign to you; you will find a babe wrapped in swaddling clothes and lying in a manger." And suddenly there was with the angel a multitude of the heavenly host praising God and saying, "Gory to God in the highest, and on earth peace among men with whom He is pleased." (Luke 2: 8-14)

When the angels went away from them into heaven, the shepherds said to one another, "Let us go to Bethlehem and see this thing that has come to pass, which the Lord has made known to us." (Luke 2: 15)

We celebrate Christmas each year on December 25th and we call it the birthday of Jesus of Nazareth, the long awaited Messiah of the Jewish Nation. Shepherds would not have been in the hills in the dead of winter when there would have been no grass for their sheep to eat. Yet, the scriptures report that at the time of the birth of Christ there were shepherds in the hills watching their flocks of sheep. Thus, we should acknowledge that no one knows exactly the date of the birth of Christ. It most likely would have been in either the fall or the spring because the shepherds would not have taken their sheep to the hills in the heat of the summer or the cold of the winter.

Today, if you visit Bethlehem and other parts of Judea you will find the shepherds still taking their sheep into the hills in the spring and fall of the year. Tourist buses often have to slow to a stop to allow herds of sheep to cross the roads on their way to the best grazing lands. One unique thing about those sheep in modern days is that they often have colored marks on their flanks that identify their ownership. One shepherd often takes care of the sheep of many owners and, thus, it is not unusual to see sheep with red, blue, green, and other color marks on their backs. It is like the practice of branding cattle in the western U.S. that helps ranchers identify which cattle are theirs when they round them up from the open range.

And they went with haste, and found Mary and Joseph, and the babe lying in a manger. And when they saw it they made known the saying which had been told them concerning this child; and all who heard it wondered at what the shepherds told them. But Mary kept all these things, pondering them in her heart. And the shepherds returned, glorifying and praising God for all they had heard and seen, as it had been told them. (Luke 2: 16-20)

THE CHRISTMAS STAR

In his Gospel, Matthew wrote that a miraculous star rose above the place where Jesus was born and dominated the Judean sky, brought the shepherds and guided the wise men who were coming from the East to see the new King.

Only Matthew wrote of the star. Mark, Luke, and John, the writers of the other Gospels, did not mention it. King Herod did not seem to know there was a new star in the Judean sky. Of course, that doesn't mean the star wasn't there but it does mean that it probably was very different from what we might imagine. The star did not become important to the people of Jerusalem until the Magi arrived and told them the importance of the star.

After Jesus was born in Bethlehem in Judea, during the time of King Herod, Magi from the east came to Jerusalem and asked, "Where is the one who has been born King of the Jews? We saw His star in the east and have come to worship Him." When King Herod heard this he was disturbed, and all Jerusalem with him. When he had called together all the people's chief priests and teachers of the law, he asked them where the Christ was to be born. "In Bethlehem in Judea," they replied, "for this is what the prophet has written." Then Herod called the Magi secretly and found out from them the exact time the star had appeared. He sent them to Bethlehem and said, "Go and make a careful search for the child. As soon as you find Him, report to me, so that I too may go and worship Him." (Matthew 2: 1-8)

After they had heard the king, they went on their way, and the star they had seen in the east went ahead of them until it stopped over the place where the child was. (Matthew 2: 9)

So, where was the star? The scriptures say that they "saw the star in the East." Actually, one might say they were in the east and that is where they saw the star. However, the Greek translation indicates that they were talking about seeing it rise in the eastern sky. It wasn't to the west of them toward Judea and Bethlehem at all.

Also, from the time they saw the star in the east it would have taken them about six weeks to travel the distance from the region of Babylon to Jerusalem.

The phrase "the star they had seen in the east went ahead of them" is only applied after they left Jerusalem and headed toward Bethlehem. Jerusalem is due north of Bethlehem. So, in order to identify what God used to create the beacon star one is looking for something that was in the sky, rising in the east but by six weeks later was in the southern sky. That is the only way the star could have seemed to be going before them when they left Jerusalem.

What was the star? One can speculate that the star was one of four things: a comet, a meteor, a constellation of planets, or a miraculous light in the sky put there specifically by God for the purpose of fulfilling the prophecy of the Oracle of Balaam from the Old Testament. Because of the circumstances of the star, the birth, the coming of the Magi, and the fact that King Herod did not know the star was there, several things must come together in order to fulfill the prophecy. It must ...

1. have happened on the date of the Nativity;

2. be a singular, special, or spectacular event;

3. be a rare even, perhaps never seen before by those present;

4. have had a special meaning for the Magi;

5. have occurred originally in the east and moved to the southern sky;

6. have endured for six to eight weeks in the sky.

One can rule out the comet and meteor because they do not have the properties described in Matthew's writing. One can never rule out a miraculous light put there by God. However, the one thing that makes sense of the natural phenomena is that of a constellation of planets.

In order to understand how such a thing could be in the sky without King Herod seeing it, but could alert the Magi of the miraculous birth of a new king in Judea and then guide them to the birth site, we have to first understand something of astrology--not astronomy, but astrology. Yes, that pseudo-science that gives you your horoscope in the newspaper every morning.

(NOTE: Insert grid of the divisions in the sky that included Pisces.)

In the astrology of the time every planet and star had a name and a purpose. And, every part of the sky was assigned to a particular country. The stars and planets located in the constellation called Pisces were associated with the Jews in Judea. Thus, anything that appeared in the sky in Pisces was judged to have something to do with the Jews. The planet Jupiter was judged to be a "royal" planet. Thus, if Jupiter was in Pisces something related to a king was going to happen in Judea. Saturn was a planet that was judged to be a negative when it was in your section of the sky. The presence of the planet Mars generally meant war.

To speculate, if one found Jupiter and Saturn close together in Pisces it could have suggested to the Magi that a great ruler (the awaited Messiah) would arise to challenge a malign one (the Roman Empire), to liberate His country by the sword (as signified by the presence of Mars).

Prior to the advent of computers there was no way for us to recreate the skies over Judea and the Middle East. Today, they can chart the motion of the heavenly bodies, reverse the movement and recreate the location of the stars and the planets as far back as 2000 years ago and more. As the science of astronomy (not astrology) tells us from the charting the skies over Judea in the year 5 B.C., there was a great gathering of planets at that time in the constellation of Pisces. Jupiter (royal) met Saturn (negative) and Mars (war) and formed a three-planet constellation. Just at this time a nova (a bright light) appeared in the sky. All of these happenings together signified to the Magi that not only was the stage set for the birth of the Messiah but the nova signified that the birth had occurred. In short, if they were going to see this great thing they would have to get on their journey.

NOTE: There is much more to the story of the star of Bethlehem. For further information please refer to a book titled *The Star of Bethlehem* which can be found in many public libraries.

THE MAGI, WISE MEN FROM THE EAST

The story of the Magi, wise men from the east, traveling to the Holy Land to worship the newborn king is one of the more heartwarming parts of the Christmas story. Who were they and where did they come from? How did they know of the birth of the Messiah? Can this story be true?

Of the four Gospel writers only Matthew told the story of the Magi who came to Bethlehem to see the Christ Child. Mark, Luke, John, Peter, and James, the brother of Jesus did not mention the Magi as a part of the story of Jesus' life.

Now when Jesus was born in Bethlehem of Judea in the days of Herod the king, behold, wise men from the East came to Jerusalem, saying "Where is he who has been born king of the Jews? For we have seen his star in the East, and have come to worship him." (Matthew 2: 1-2)

So, who were the Magi? Biblical scholars have speculated for centuries as to who they were. It has been assumed that they were astrologers, learned men, kings from the Tigress and Euphrates River Valleys where science was far advanced over that of the Holy Land.

Discoveries made recently by archeologists in Iraq have provided some new information. Evidently, there was an ancient king who had a court made up of men called Magoi. The Magoi were evidently war lords from the region, each ruling a section of the kingdom and coming together from time to time to advise the king on matters of state. According to the scriptures in Daniel, Ezra, and Nehemiah, that is consistent with how the Persians ruled their empire between 605 B.C. and 400 B.C. It is also consistent with what we have learned in recent years in countries such as Afghanistan, Yemen, and Somalia. War lords still exist in those middle-eastern countries. If the Magoi are, in fact, the Magi of the Bible they were war lords, and kings in their own right. Each would have had his own kingdom and his own army. Of course, we need more information on this finding before totally accepting it. Still, it does seem to fit the story.

How did the Magi get to the Holy Land? It is likely that they traveled up the Tigress and Euphrates River valleys and then crossed over toward Mount Hermon and came down through Galilee to Jerusalem. Coming straight across, east to west, from the region of Babylon to Jerusalem would have taken them through more than three hundred miles of impassable desert lands. The following is pure speculation but makes sense as per the story in the scriptures. The Magi would have traveled by horseback on those beautiful Arabian horses of which they are still so proud. Camels are beasts of burden and used primarily for carrying cargo and goods. It is not likely that a king would have been riding on a camel. Further, it is likely that the kings would have brought along their militia for protection. Each king might have brought as many as three hundred soldiers with them. Their army, with soldiers and supporters, might have been as many as a thousand or more. Thus, it was prudent to go first to see Herold, the King of Judea, to announce their arrival and state their intentions. Otherwise, Herod might have thought they had sinister motives for coming into his kingdom with such an army.

During their trip, there is no mention of the star they had seen in the east. Thus, it is likely they lost sight of it. Had they been following it they might have gone directly to Bethlehem since the star would have guided them on a route several miles south of Jerusalem.

Whether or not they had lost sight of the star, it is proper protocol for a visiting king to announce his presence in the kingdom of another and to state his purpose for being there. That is a good explanation as to why they went first to see King Herod in Jerusalem. Imagine their surprise when Herod did not even know of the star that had motivated them to take this very difficult journey.

When Herod the king heard this, he was troubled, and all Jerusalem with him; and assembling all the chief priests and scribes of the people, he inquired of them where the Christ was to be born. They told him, "In Bethlehem of Judea; for so it is written by the prophet: The prophet said, 'And you, O Bethlehem, in the land of Judah, are by no means least among the rulers of Judah; for from you shall come a ruler who will govern my people Israel." (Mathew 2: 3-6)

These words created anguish in the mind of Herod. He had been ruling for many years at that time and, due to his age, probably did not have much concern for his future. However, he had sons to succeed him on the throne in Judea. Herod Antipas was next in line to become king and if a rival for the throne had been born in Bethlehem it might threaten the Herod family line of control. Thus, he was very interested in this new baby born in Bethlehem who, according to the prophets, would be king.

Then Herod summoned the wise men secretly and ascertained from them what time the star appeared; and he sent them to Bethlehem, saying, "Go and search diligently for the child, and when you have found him bring me word, that I too may come and worship him." When they had heard the king they went their way; and lo, the star which they had seen in the East went before them, till it came to rest over the place where the child was. (Matthew 2: 7-9)

The wise men listened to what Herod said but they saw the evil in his heart. When they turned south from the palace at Jerusalem they could again see the star.

When they saw the star they rejoiced exceedingly with great joy. (Matthew 2: 10)

The scriptures tell us that the star that they had seen in the east six to eight weeks before was now in the southern sky because Bethlehem is directly south of Jerusalem. That change of location in a six-week period helps to identify what God had used to create the bright beacon in the sky.

And going into the house they saw the child with Mary His mother, and they fell down and worshiped Him. Then opening their treasures, they offered Him gifts, gold and frankincense and myrrh. (Matthew 2: 11)

Six weeks had passed since they first saw the star and the nova, the flash of light in the night sky, that signaled the birth of the baby. The little family was no longer in the stable with the baby lying in a manger. Evidently, most of the visitors to Bethlehem had paid their taxes and gone home and so there was now ample room for the little family in a house. Joseph, Mary and the baby were still in Bethlehem to fulfill the two-month waiting period that was traditional following the birth of a baby.

The number of the gifts raises the question as to how many kings were in the traveling party. Tradition has always said there were three, primarily because they gave three gifts. There might have been more kings in the group, or fewer. The scriptures don't tell us.

And being warned in a dream not to return to Herod, they departed to their own country by another way. (Matthew 2: 12)

Now when they had departed, behold, an angel of the Lord appeared to Joseph in a dream and said, "Rise, take the child and His mother, and flee to Egypt, and remain there till I tell you; for Herod is about to search for the child, to destroy Him: And he rose and took the child and His mother by night, and departed to Egypt, and remained there until the death of Herod. (Matthew 2: 13-14)

PEACE THROUGH RELIGIOUS UNDERSTANDING

None of us who have spent our lives involved in a search for God have any doubt as to the importance of religion in everyday life. Religion is important all around the globe and because it is we need to study and understand the various forms of religion, faiths other than our own, and the importance of these various faiths for promoting understanding, friendships, and, ultimately, world peace.

There are more than four hundred identifiable religions practiced in the world today. Five of these are generally referred to us as "major" because of the importance of the religion in history and the number of devotees who practice their tenets. The five are, in order of their origin in the world, Hinduism, Judaism, Christianity, Buddhism, and Islam. Hinduism and Buddhism both had their start in south Asia in the northern part of present-day India. Judaism, Christianity, and Islam all came from a common seed in western Asia in the present-day country of Israel.

Many of us have friendships that have formed across religious lines among people of many faiths. Indeed, in a family business that serves an international clientele the author has partners in Asia who are Buddhist, Hindu, Muslim, and Jewish, as well as Christian. Religious discussions are a usual part of our relationship with them. These relationships should help us deepen our faith since people who do not believe as we do prod us into a closer examination of the tenets of our own faith. The more we understand about their faiths the more we understand our own.

We human beings are, fundamentally, religious creatures. Our response to our religious impulse is either to worship God or to worship something that is less than God. As Christian author C.S. Lewis observed; "What Satan put into the head of our remote ancestors was the idea that they could be like gods, could set up on their own as if they had created themselves, be their own master, invent some sort of happiness for themselves outside God, apart from God. And, out of that hopeless attempt has come nearly all that we can identify as the foundations of human misery--money, poverty, ambition, war, prostitution, classes, empires, slavery—the long terrible story of man trying to find something other than God which will make him happy."

At our best, however, we worship God, the Supreme Being. It is the same on remote mountain peaks and broad prairies, in jungles and deserts, in rural outposts and in the midst of our largest cities, humans worship the divine. And, despite the variety of their geographical beginnings and the diversity of their followers, different religions all have certain essential elements in common.

Whether Hindu or Christian, Buddhist, Muslim or Jew, it is our religion that gives us direction, a sense of self-worth, and a feeling of oneness with the universe. It is our faith that undergirds our morality. Our religious beliefs prompt us to acts of genuine altruism. People of every religious group abandon the comforts of home and family and travel great distances to meet the needs of those less fortunate. Through the financial contributions of the faithful, the hungry are fed, the homeless are housed, and the naked are clothed. The imperatives of religious belief send men and women all over the world to minister to those in need.

One of the common sayings in all religions is, "Prayer changes things." For the believer prayer has power to alter physical circumstance. Studies show that people who pray, and are prayed for, experience better medical outcomes than those who do not pray and for whom no prayers are offered.

No religion teaches that it is good to steal, to murder, or to be vicious. Violence and war are aberrations of our faiths, yet each faith's tradition has the capacity for destruction. Christians have been a part of the Crusades, slavery, the Holocaust, apartheid, and the Ku Klux Klan. Hindus were responsible for the bloody expulsion of Muslims to Pakistan at the time of partition in 1947. Jews raze the homes of Palestinians and mount raids on refugee camps. Muslims waged holy wars into Byzantium, Persia, North Africa, and Spain and today some Muslims strap munitions to their bodies and become suicide bombers.

All faiths have the potential to create saints and breed fanatics. Hinduism brought us the wisdom of Gandhi and the madness of his assassin. Buddhism has shown us the tranquil face of the Dalai Lama in Tibet and the brutality of Pol Pot in Cambodia. Judaism has given us the courage of young Anne Frank and the insanity of fundamentalist Baruch Goldstein. Christianity was the religion of both Mother Theresa and of Adolf Hitler. Islam was the faith of the poet Rumi and the terrorist Osama bin Laden.

Yet it is also within each faith that the paths to redemption lie. It was Christianity that sustained America's slaves and motivated her abolitionists. The oppressed under South Africa's apartheid were sustained by their Christian faith and it was Christians, Muslims, and Jews who came together to become the leaders of the anti-apartheid struggle. It was men and women of all faiths who had the courage to oppose the Nazi Holocaust.

Each religion offers a path to God. We can benefit by hearing what members of other faiths have to say about their seeking God. In their exploration we may find the keys to doors heretofore closed against us. Contrary to our own scripture, Christians have been quick to dismiss the notion that other faiths have any insights into truth and have been content to remain ignorant of the beliefs of other religions. Yet the God who created us is bigger than any single religion. The paths to the knowledge of God may be many more than we can imagine. God is too big to fit into our box.

In our minds we are the center of the universe. Yet, poverty, war, injustice, and oppression are born from human self-centeredness. In the world of yesterday, today, and tomorrow human beings are not the center of the universe. God is.

Religion is the hope of the world for peace because each religion forces us to look beyond our own personal wants and needs, beyond our local or national aspirations to the service of a God who is greater than we are. All the major religions look forward to a time when all creation is reunited with the divine. All look forward to a time when goodness will prevail over evil; when hope will overcome fear; when light will banish the darkness; when joy will dry every tear; when justice will be as a flood to drown injustice and oppression, and God, the Supreme, will, indeed, be the great I Am.

(With thanks to Bishop Desmond Tutu of South Africa for an article that helped shape my thinking on this essay.)

THE READERS

The author sincerely appreciates the advice and counsel of three who contributed their best thoughts to this manuscript. In any presentation of Biblical topics there is always opportunity for disagreement and controversy. In order to reduce that possibility to the extent possible, three highly qualified ministers were asked to read portions of this manuscript that relate directly to the Bible and raise concerns or suggest changes with the content. Their best thoughts and comments were incorporated into the text. Still, the responsibility for the content belongs solely to the author. The following is an introduction to the three readers.

Reverend Jack Ellenburg: Reverend Ellenburg is a graduate of Furman University in South Carolina, the University of Louisville, and Southern Seminary in Louisville, KY. He has a diverse history of education and Christian service including Connie Maxwell Children's Home, Piedmont Technical College, and the Southern Baptist Home Mission Board. He was pastor of six Southern Baptist churches during his forty-plus-year career and retired from Riverland Hills Baptist Church in Columbia, SC. Reverend Ellenburg served the South Carolina Baptist Convention Board as an executive committee member, was twice chairman of Associational Pastors Conferences, and was chairman of the board of Anderson University. He served for several years as a consultant to the Life Support for Pastors program for the SCBC. He most recently served as associate pastor and administrator of Concord Baptist Church in Anderson, SC. He currently is retired in Anderson and continues to teach at Concord.

Doctor Paul Talmadge: Dr. Talmadge is a graduate of Samford University in Birmingham, AL and Southwestern Theological Seminary in Fort Worth, TX. He taught New Testament and served as campus minister at Samford before moving to North Greenville College in South Carolina. There he taught Old and New Testament and served as academic dean. In 1969 Dr. Talmadge became vice president for academic affairs at Anderson College, a post he held for nineteen years before becoming president of North Greenville College in 1988. In 1991 he became training coordinator for the Billy Graham Center in Black Mountain, NC. Dr. Talmadge is currently retired and living in Anderson, SC.

Doctor Randall Ruble: Dr. Ruble is a graduate of Erskine College and Erskine Seminary in Due West, SC. He also holds degrees from Princeton Theological Seminary in NJ and the University of Edinburgh in Scotland. He has done additional graduate study at the University of Goettingen in Germany, Harvard University's School of Theology, and the Center of Theological Inquiry at Princeton. He returned to Erskine to teach Hebrew and Old Testament and to serve as chaplain of the college. He then served as dean of the seminary, vice president, and then president of Erskine College. He has served as chairman of many committees of accreditation for the Southern Association of Colleges and Schools and the Association of Theological Schools. Dr. Ruble is retired and lives in Due West, SC. (You can read comments from Dr. Ruble on the back cover of this book.)

EXHIBITS IN THE BACK OF THE BOOK

I envision a section of maps in color at the end of the book that will provide additional reference material for the reader. Multiple references to the maps are included in the text of the manuscript, especially in the section related to geography. I have found the maps needed on the Internet but do not know if they are restricted by copyright. The proposed cover is also included though there may be a better cover idea among the professionals. This one was created by my wife who is a professional artist. I am not adept enough in the world of computers to send you the exhibits or cover by computer so, when it is appropriate, I will send them by snail mail.

A list of exhibits follows:

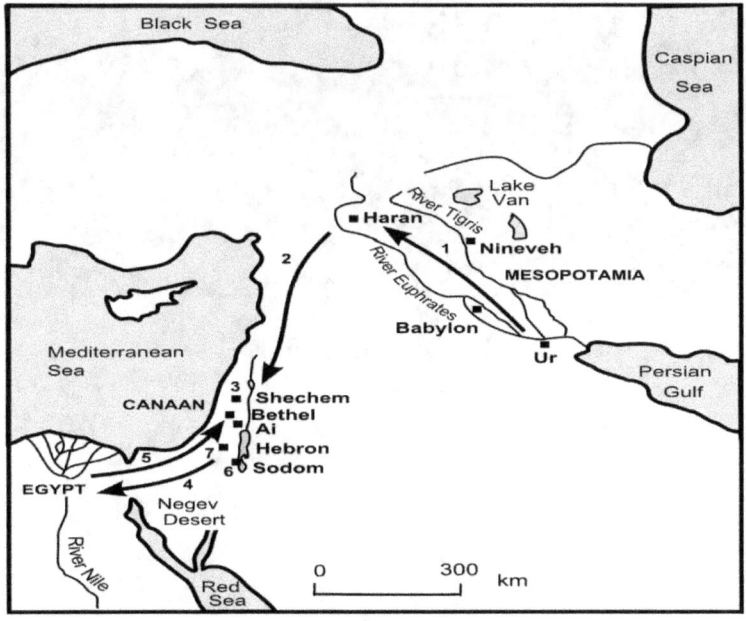

Abraham's Journey

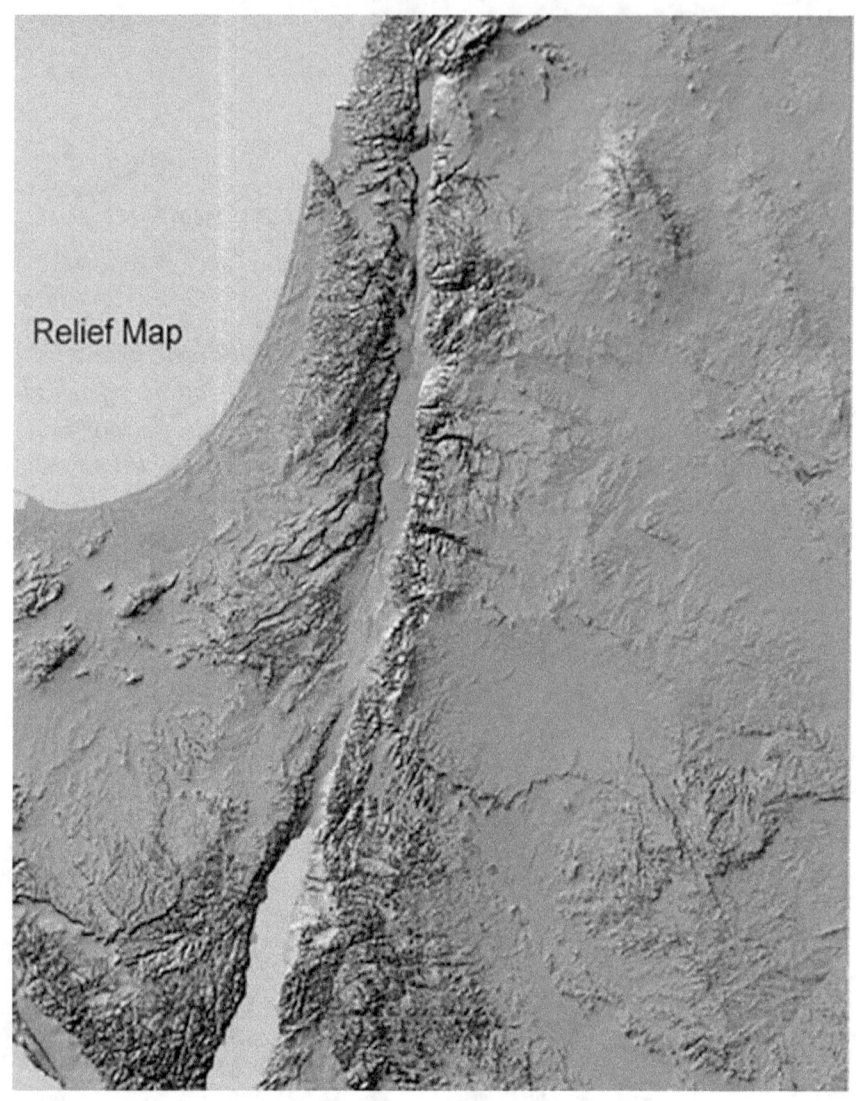

The Dead Sea Rift, 1.

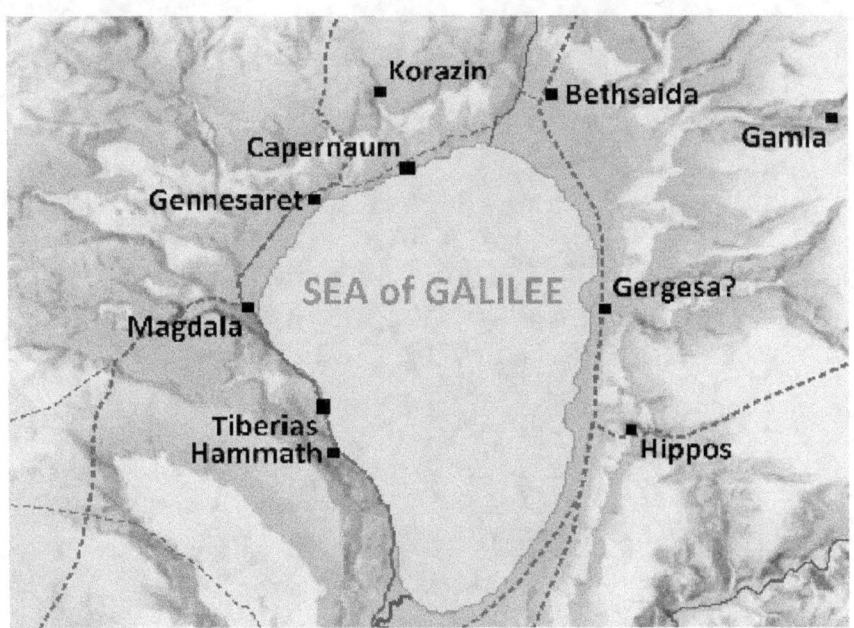

The Sea of Galilee

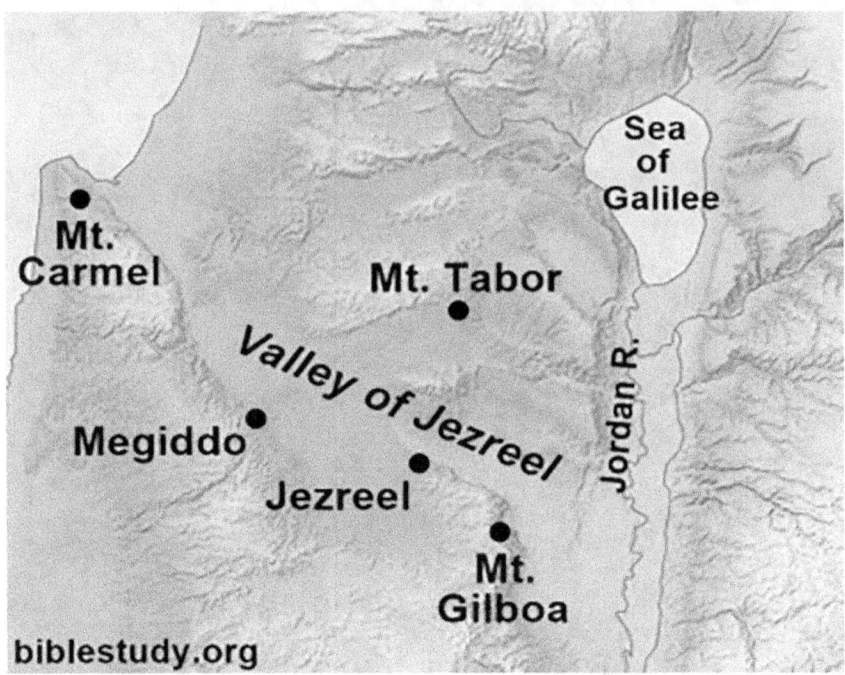

The Jordan River Valley & Jezreel Valley

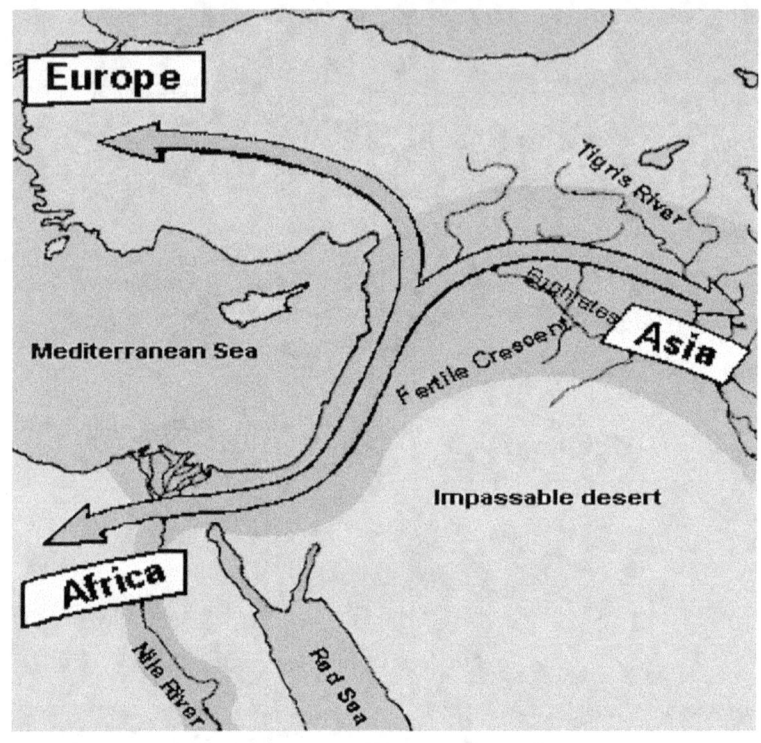

Trade Routes of the Mid-East

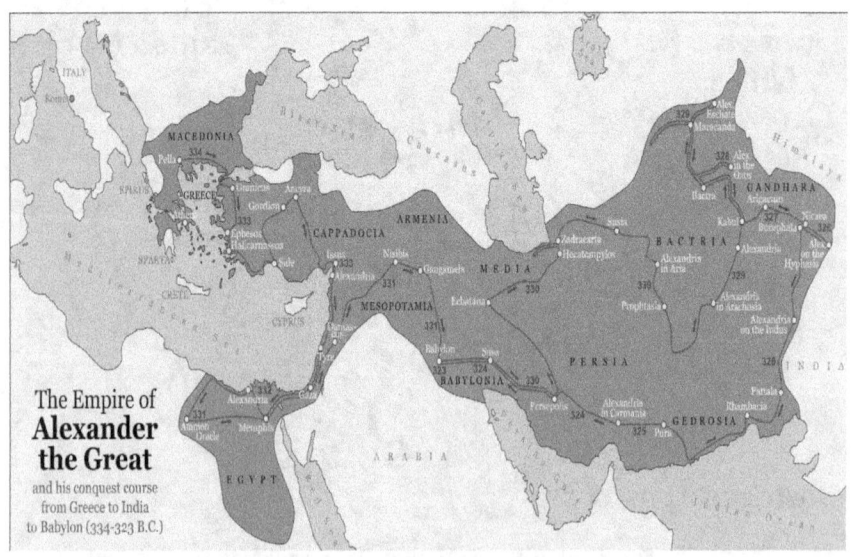

Alexander the Great's Empire

The Roman Empire

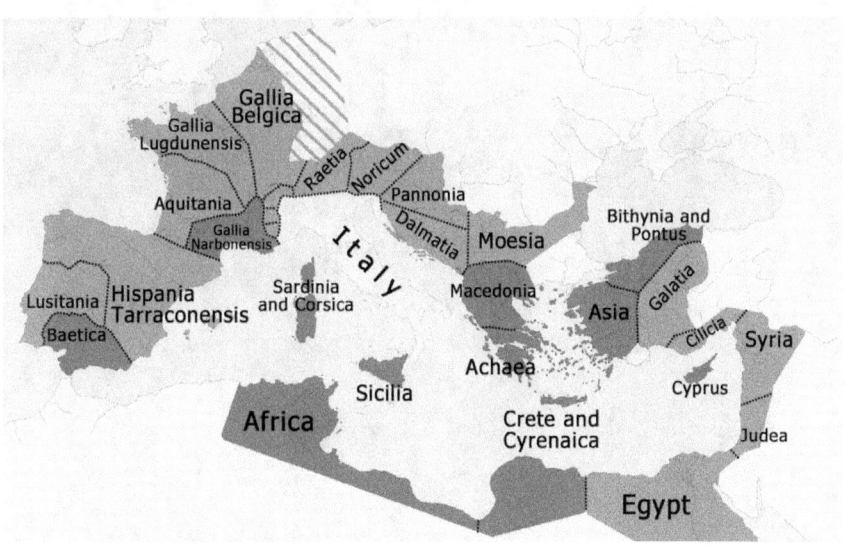

The Roman Provinces

Ancient Macedonia

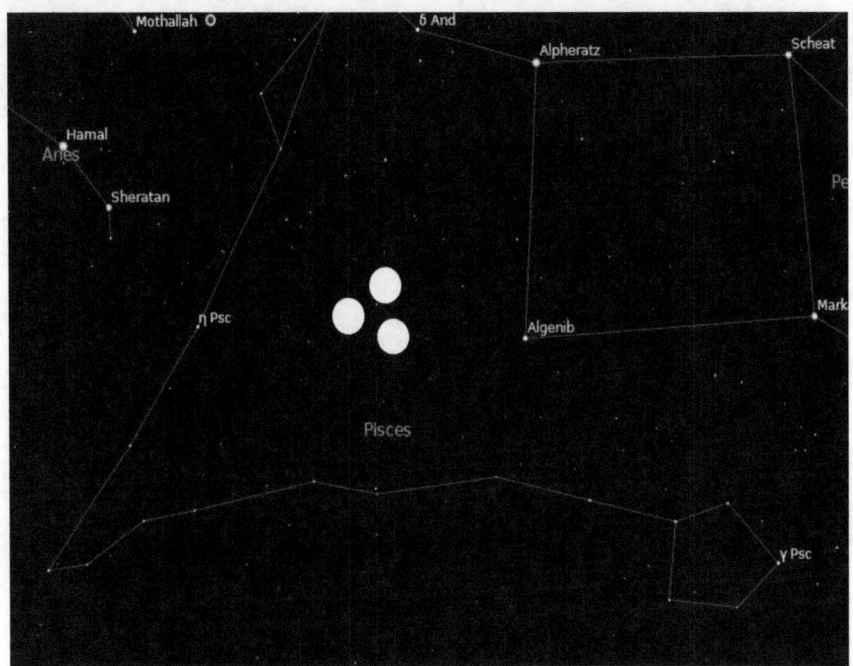

The night sky with the Jupiter, Saturn gathering near Pisces

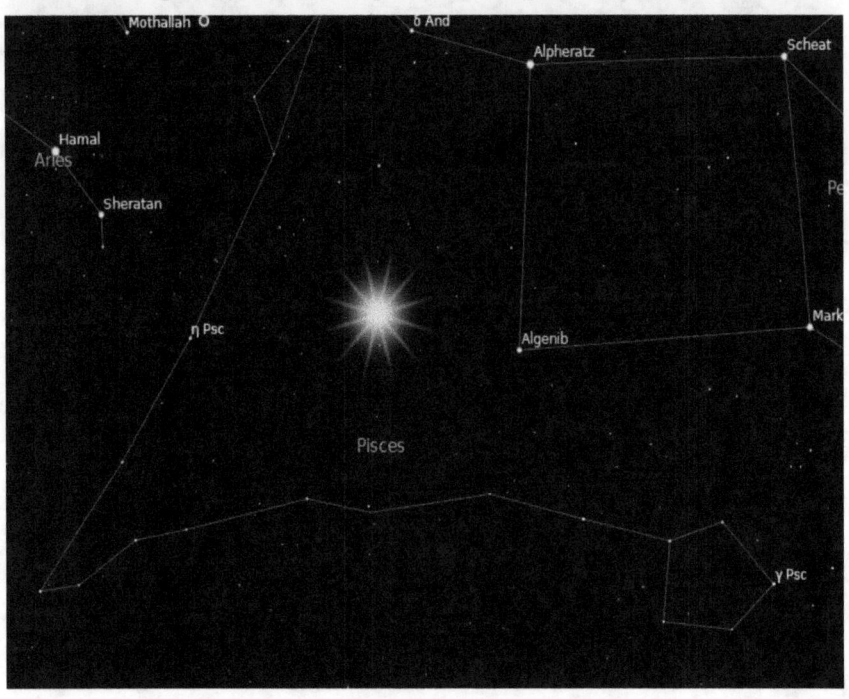

Jupiter, Saturn, and Mars together in Pisces

THE AUTHOR

Dr. Mark L. Hopkins was president of four institutions of higher education over a forty year career, including Anderson (Baptist) University in Anderson, SC. He holds three degrees from Missouri universities and taught history and psychology before moving into university administration. Dr. Hopkins has served as a Sunday school teacher, Sunday school superintendent, deacon, minister of music, and pastor as well as teaching a number of Bible- related courses over the years. Dr. Hopkins has taught *New Testament, Old Testament, Miracles and Mysteries of the Bible, In the Footsteps of Paul the Apostle, Comparative Religion, and The World as It Was When Jesus Came.* It was this last course that served as the prime motivator for writing this book.